BEST
of the
OLD NORTHWEST

TRUE STORIES, ANECDOTES, LEGENDS AND MYSTERIES OF THOSE EXCITING EARLY YEARS.

By Marge Davenport

BEST of the OLD NORTHWEST

Published By: **PADDLEWHEEL PRESS**
15100 S.W. 109th
Tigard, Oregon 97223 U.S.A.

Printed in the United States of America

Library of Congress cataloging in Publication Data
Davenport, Marge E., date

ISBN No. 0-938274-00-7
Library of Congress Catalog Card No. 80-83780

FOREWORD

The real romance and color of the Old Northwest is not found in history book texts. The characters, the funny incidents, the legends and the mysteries are what make the first 175 years of Northwest history exciting and fun.

For the past five years, the publishers of "OLD STUFF," the Northwest quarterly on antiques, collectibles, history and nostalgia, have been gathering these stories and they have become so much in demand that we decided to put them in book form so they could be shared by more people.

They are the stories of a rugged people — you had to be rugged if you came to the Northwest in the early days. The trip was long and dangerous whether you came cross-country by wagon or sailed around the Horn. For almost the first 100 years there was no law in the Northwest Territory and little law enforcement. Indians were friendly one minute, scalping you the next. Survival was difficult.

Needless to say, all these things spawned great stories and good story tellers. They lived hard and developing a good sense of humor was necessary. Change came fast as they moved from the most primitive of conditions of the early West to catch up with the rest of the world. Finding gold speeded the tempo, and added yarns as rich as nuggets.

Discovering the colorful stories of the Northwest's past has been exciting, educational and fun. We hope you enjoy "The Best of the Old Northwest" as much as we enjoyed putting it together for you.

Marge Davenport

FOR THE RECORD

Without the efforts of Morton Spence and Lydge Cady, the other two-thirds of Paddlewheel Press enterprises, this book would not have been possible.

All three of us would also like to express special thanks to Tom and Marcia Pry at the Bee who have held our hand through all our publication struggles and have offered sympathy and guidance; to Linda Schwartz, who does many of our illustrations, and especially, we would like to thank everyone who has contributed to, or supported OLD STUFF, our quarterly publication, because the stories which have appeared in it made this book possible.

CONTENTS

LOST GOLD LAKE

Golden Lake Still There?

Somewhere in the North Cascade Mountains there may be a marvelous lake whose banks are lined with gold nuggets.

It must still be there, because a captain in the U.S. Cavalry discovered it in 1872 and brought out samples of the gold to prove his story. However, he was killed shortly thereafter in a shooting accident and no one has been able to find the lake or the map that the captain said he drew and buried.

Capt. Ben Ingalls estimated that there were about 10 tons of gold in view above ground in the crumbling quartz around the lake shore. By our reckoning (320 ounces per ton, at $600 per ounce), that would make about $192 million worth of gold on today's market. He speculated that there was probably much more hidden in the lake and in the ground around the lake.

Alone With Discovery

The captain said he discovered the canyon and the fabulous lake after he became separated from members of his scouting party and was lost in the formidable wilderness of the Cascades in 1872.

He reached a mountaintop along a narrow ridge and, looking into the canyon below, discovered that it held three small lakes connected by a narrow stream. Two of the lakes looked dark and deep, but the middle one was crescent shaped and shimmering green.

Following a game trail, he reached the floor of the canyon and was amazed at what he saw. The crescent-shaped lake had a beach of crumbling quartz rock thickly studded with glittering gold.

Captain Mapped Area

Forgetting about his troops, Capt. Ingalls stayed in the canyon about two days and as he left, he carefully drew a map of the entire area, which he said was near Mt. Stuart (south-west of what is now Wenatchee).

On his way out he followed the creek which now bears his name. For safe-keeping, he buried the map somewhere near the mouth of the creek before he started looking for the rest of his scouting party.

Capt. Ingalls spent the next night several miles from the canyon, and was awakened by the shrill screams of his horse. Earthquake! The ground under him shook violently and the mountains rumbled. He heard boulders crash, and trees splinter, but he was unhurt and didnt't realize until later that he was experiencing the great earthquake of 1872.

Death Stops Search

After the captain found his troops, he wrote to a friend, J. Hansel, telling him about his discovery and sending samples of the gold. He asked Hansel to join him at the mouth on Ingalls Creek, saying they would return to the lake together. But before that hapened, Ingalls met death accidentally.

Hansel spent years looking for the lake, but never was able to find it or the map.

Did the earthquake bury the multimillion dollar lake? Or is it still shimmering at the bottom of some remote canyon in the North Cascades? No one knows.

●

Streets Paved With Gold

If the price of gold keeps escalating, someone may be filing a claim and mining the streets of Cottage Grove!

In 1935, Cottage Grove's "streets of gold" were cited in Ripley's "Believe It Or Not." The story goes back to 1900, when a contractor hauled rock from the Row River to put on the city streets. The local doctor, who had a keen interest in mining, had the rock being spread on the city streets in the paving assayed, and found that it carried a small percentage of gold.

Scientists and chemists consulted at the time claimed that gold of the character found continues to "grow" though they were careful to say the process is slow. In the course of a few thousand years, Cottage Grove's streets should be solid gold.

Ripley said Cottage Grove was probably "the only town in the world with streets paved with gold!" ●

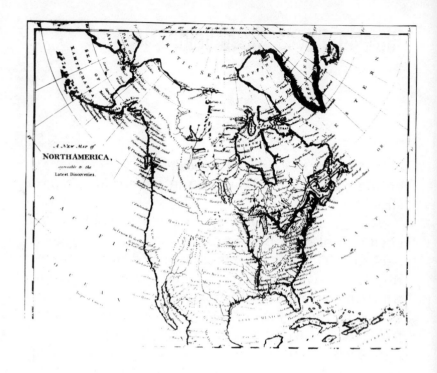

On maps of the 1500's and 1600's, Quivira was shown as the large area south of the ''River of the West'' (not yet named Columbia River.) The fabulous City of Quivira was not shown on maps, but was reportedly along the coast because from there trade was carried on with China. Early residents of Curry County believed they had found lost City of Quivira.

Rich Mythical Kingdom in Oregon?

The Northwest has its own "Camelot," a romantic and mythical kingdom duly recorded in old history books and old maps, but like King Arthur's kingdom, its exact location cannot be pinpointed, or its existence verified.

The mysterious kingdom of Quivira was vaguely located on the west coast of North America, somewhere near the southern part of Oregon. Some say Oregon's Sixes River was its northern boundary.

For over 200 years, Quivira was shown on all maps, charts, atlases and globes. It was on Mercator's Map in 1569, and continued to be shown on maps in 1570, 1582, 1592, 1597, 1600, 1630, 1637, 1671 and as late as 1750.

Ruled by a "long-bearded, hoary-headed fellow named Tatarrax," Quivira was reputed to be a fabulous kingdom with great wealth and prosperity.

One record discusses the kingdom's trade with China, and reports a Chinese ship in the harbor of the City of Quivira, which it says was located on a bay at the mouth of a big river.

Further up the river was another important city called Tuchano, according to this report.

At the time Quivira was supposedly a great kingdom, Spain controlled the seas, and claimed all of the west coast of North America by right of discovery and exploration. Spain also traded extensively with China at this time, and was building ships at Panama.

Some historical records indicate that the King of

Spain wanted to keep the existence of Quivira a Spanish secret, and this is why so little was recorded about it. Other histories say that countless explorers looked in vain for the reportedly rich Quivira, but found only poor native settlements.

Some stories say that Phillip III of Spain discovered among his father's secret papers "a sworn declaration that a foreigner had given him telling about visiting the populous and rich city named Quivira."

It was believed that the river on the West Coast of North America discovered and recorded by the Spanish explorer Martin d'Agulai was the one leading to the great city of Quivira, but this river could never be located definitely by later navigators.

(This author found frequent references to the kingdom of Quivira in old books at the University of California library in Berkeley, and records of Spanish expeditions seeking the kingdom, but found no records pinpointing its exact location.)

In the 1880's there was a flurry of excitement around Gold Beach, Oregon, and it was believed that one of the great cities of Quivira had been located. A storm in the fall of 1881 uprooted a large spruce tree near Flores Creek. The whole root system was lifted up like the lid of a box, and underneath were cut stones "bearing quite plainly the marks of the stone cutter's chisel."

The excited discoverers decided these were part of a tumbled down wall. After the hewn sandstones were discovered, more digging was done in the area and around other mounds and many more relics of ancient masonry were found.

The Flores diggers and neighbors who joined in, also found "what to all appearances had been a mining ditch coming along the hill slope and walled up on the lower side." This ditch was made of stones similar to the others.

This archaeological find was written up in the Port Orford Post, with the editor saying he intended to personally visit the site and evaluate it. Whether or not he published more follow-up later is not known as the paper burned and the files of the Post no longer exist. The Post's original report is preserved because it was reprinted in a Portland magazine.

The author recently visited Curry County and with a great deal of difficulty finally located the old Cox homestead on Flores Creek where the stones were reputedly found in the 1880's. No one living in the area today remembers anything about the discovery however. Local residents did report that the site was known locally as the location of a large Indian village dating back to pre-settlement days.

The Curry County Museum at Gold Beach had no records of Quivira, but did have the name of the woman whose family had homesteaded the old Cox place on Flores Creek. She is over 100 years old, and could not be located for questioning.

So the mystery remains to be added to the other mysteries of the West Coast. Was Quivira somehow tied into the mystery of all the beeswax found on the coast by early settlers and explorers? Perhaps if they worked gold, the wax was used in the lost wax technique for gold castings. Gold was mined around Gold Beach after the white man came, perhaps earlier it was the source of the riches of Quivira.

Where did the metals that the Indians had when early explorers arrived come from? Were they remnants of a forgotten era, or were they brought by even earlier explorers?

What happened to the Kingdom of Quivira, if indeed, it did exist? ●

At the tables down at Erickson's there was always plenty of action. Card room off main club room attracted sailors, loggers and was second home to many workingmen.

Oregon Really Had Free Lunch

The saying goes: "There's no such thing as a free lunch." But people in the Northwest can say right back that there used to be!

The place was the famous "Workingman's Club," or Erickson's Place, and in the 1880s and for 40 ensuing years, Portland was better known as the home of Erickson's than as the City of Roses.

Erickson's was reputed to be "the longest bar in the world," and its fame has been documented by Stewart Holbrook and others who recalled its elegance and magnificence, and the bounteous "Dainty Lunch" that was served free each day.

Located on West Burnside Street, it occupied most of the block and its five great bars ran around and across from 2nd to 3rd Avenues, a total of 684 feet.

But the place offered much more. It was furnished with the best of everything. There was a concert stage, a $5,000 pipe organ and booths for ladies on the mezzanine. (No female was ever allowed on the hallowed main floor.)

It was decorated with art that was much admired by its patrons. There were elegant and classical nudes and a great oil painting, "The Slave Market," depicting the auction of Roman captives.

Founded in the early 1880s by August Erickson, an immigrant from Finland, the fame of the Workingman's Club spread among loggers, miners and around the Seven Seas, until there was always a rush for Erickson's whenever a ship docked or a train arrived. It was said that any logger that you wanted to reach would eventually show up at Erickson's, and there was always a stack of mail waiting to be claimed by persons who had no other address.

Order at Erickson's was kept by its own staff of able bouncers. The head bouncer was deceptively mild-looking, but packed a mean right. Another bouncer topped the scales at over 300 pounds and "had the appearance of an ill-natured orangutan," according to reports.

The "Dainty" free lunch consisted of slices of roast prime rib, stacks of bread, cut exactly 1½ inches thick, sliced sausage, an assortment of good cheeses, and pickled herring. Beer was 5 cents for a 16 fluid ounce schooner, Dublin porter was 5 cents a glass and all hard liquor was two for a quarter.

The 'Floating Erickson's'

During the great flood of 1894, which left much of Portland looking like Venice, Erickson hired a big houseboat and stocked it completely with all the provisions of the regular house, including the Dainty Lunch. Customers came in boats, on rafts, and quite a few loggers arrived riding big fir logs. Some stayed for the duration of the flood.

The bartenders, all giants of men, had roached.

AUGUST ERICKSON

hair and mustasches. They wore white vests with heavy gold watch chains, white shirts and neat aprons. Their elastic arm bands were the color of their choice and was the only part of their costume left to personal taste. Some wore pink, some red, and a few had purple arm bands. All wore suspenders, and they were known for their courtesy and their ability to converse on any subject with a fair amount of knowledge. When needed, they offered advice and sympathy.

Erickson's lasted for 40 years. Prohibition didn't close it, but it turned into a half-hearted place that served "near-beer," and the free lunch ended. Finally the paintings were sold, and so was the big pipe organ. The bar was cut in half. Then August Erickson died in 1925, in mid-prohibition, and the place was closed.

Today, there is an Erickson's, but its glamour is gone, and it is only a ghost of the past glory of the Workingman's Club. ●

"One-eyed Charlie" drove stagecoach on the first overland link between Portland and Sacramento. The 710-mile trip took passengers six days. Stages left both cities at 6:00 a.m., carrying mail, baggage, and sometimes large shipments of gold. The drivers all had the reputation of being tough and rugged—especially Charlie.

"One-Eyed Charlie" Fooled Them All

A West Coast woman cast a ballot in 1868 — years before women got the vote — and it was counted!

One of the more notorious stage coach drivers on the Oregon-California Line between Sacramento and Portland was "One-eyed Charlie" Pankhurst.

Credited with thwarting an attempt to hold up his stage and take the Wells Fargo cash cargo, "Charlie" also had the reputation of losing at least one days work each month from the effects of a payday hangover.

Regular passengers on the line said the increase in the wad of chewing tobacco in Charlie's cheek was a never-fail indication of rough road or trouble ahead.

When Parkhurst died in 1879, after more than 30 years of driving the stage, it was discovered that the stager was a woman! Her personal papers showed that her name was Charlotte. Since she had cast a ballot in 1868, she holds the distinction of being the first U.S. woman to vote.

Her tombstone in the Odd Fellows Cemetery at Watsonville, California, bears the name of Charley Darkey Parkhurst, 1812-1879, but the inscription says:

"Noted whip of the Gold Rush Days . . . Death revealed "One-eyed Charlie" to be a woman . . . the first woman to vote in the U.S. November 3, 1868."●

"Salem" Means Peace?

Salem means "peace," but the history of Oregon's state capital shows that peace has not always reigned in the city that sits astride Mill Creek in the Willamette Valley.

The burning of state government buildings in 1855 during the controversy about whether Salem should remain the capital gave Salem a less than peaceful start.

Earlier, the Indian name for the location of the present city at the confluence of Mill Creek and the Willamette River was "Chemeketa," according to McArthur's "Oregon Geographic Names." It meant "meeting place," or "resting place."

When a Mission institute was built at Chemeketa in 1841, the location became known as "Mill" (because of Mill Creek) or "The Institute." Following the abandonment of the mission in 1844, a township was laid out on the grounds.

No one is sure just who chose the name Salem for the new township, although some contend that it was David Leslie, a trustee of the town who came from Salem, Massachusetts.

In December, 1853, a fight raged in the territorial legislature about changing the name of Salem to Thurston, Velena or to Corvallis. The names Chemawa and Willamette were also debated, but all failed and the name Corvallis went to a rival city in the valley. Salem was destined to remain Salem, the anglicized form of the Hebrew word Shalom, meaning peace.

For more than 15 years after a state government was formed, there continued to be many battles about the location of the Oregon capital. The first legislative assembly met at Oregon City in 1844. By an act of 1851, the capital was moved to Salem, but in 1855, it was moved to Corvallis. When Salem supporters managed to get it moved back to Salem later the same year, the burning of the capital buildings was reported to be a part of the controversy.

Even after Salem became firmly entrenched as the state's capital city, peace has not always reigned. Many bitter battles rage that often resound around the state during each legislative session, and there has continued to be a struggle with minor skirmishes periodically about whether all the state agencies should be headquartered in Salem.

Opposing those who believe Salem should be a "total capital" are others who contend that certain agencies which deal in services to people should stay in the Portland metropolitan area where the majority of the state's population resides.

This battle is frequently refought, but so far, the State Health Commission, the Department of Geology, the Board of Nursing, the Board of Pharmacy and a few other departments have successfully managed to remain in Portland.

However, residents of Salem, where usually only during legislative sessions do hustle and bustle and controversy take over, will tell you that Salem is a peaceful place, just as its name indicates. ●

Columbia Stopped Flowing in 1872!

Suddenly, in 1872, the Columbia River stopped flowing! It was a quiet, calm night when the big earthquake hit the North Cascades. To the few residents, the travelers and the Indians in the area, it seemed that the world was coming to an end.

The ground rocked and shook as if it was going to buck the few little cabins of the pioneers off the face of the earth. Trees swayed and snapped. Dogs howled, and the screams of terified Indians echoed through their camps. A family near where the town of Entiat, Wash., would be founded, testified in family records to the severity of the quake. The rumbling, roaring noise that accompanied the quake was deafening, they said.

Then, just as the quake began to subside and the noise stopped, there was a deafening roar, as if the surrounding mountains were collapsing.

Indeed, that was exactly what was happening. The mountain just north of the family's cabin, composed of granite interlaced with layers of volcanic ash, had split in half, and millions of tons of rocks and earth crashed thousands of feet below into the mighty Columbia River — to become an earth dam blocking its flow!

Because there were few residents in the area, and because those who had settled there lived in small frame wooden buildings, there were no casualties recorded the night of the big quake, but many strange things were reported.

When Indian women went to the river to get water

the next morning from their camp near Wenatchee, they found the river had dried up and vanished.

A Yakima pioneer said two large cracks had opened up along a ridge east of the Columbia River and oil was pouring out of the cracks and running down the mountain.

At Lake Wenatchee, where a pack train carrying supplies to a railroad survey party was camped, the packers reported huge boulders rumbled down Dirty Face Mountain and plunged into the lake.

At another spot, this near Chelan Landing, a huge geyser shot high into the air, and continued to flow for months before its pressure was reduced and it became a mere spring. The Columbia River's flow continued to be dammed for several days and everyone within traveling distance came to see the phenomenon. Fortunately, when the dam finally began to weaken and burst, those ahead of the wall of water that rushed down the valley were able to scurry to safety.

No Effect at Portland?

At Portland, there is no recorded effect of the damming of the Columbia, although when the dam burst, it must have had some influence on the water level downstream. However, persons living along the river at that time built well back from the shores because of frequent flooding and even a significant difference in water levels probably was not unusual.

Besides, the Snake, the Yakima, the John Day, the Deschutes, and other large rivers join the Columbia before it reaches Portland, so the river probably just dropped slowly for several days and then surged as if from snow melt or cloudburst when the dam water was released.

Severe earthquakes were evidently more frequent in the Northwest in the 1800s, but because there were no recording instruments, because population was sparse, and communication was mostly by word of mouth, reports are vague as to their exact intensity. The next year after the North Cascades quake that dammed the Columbia River, a severe quake was reported at Ft. Klamath to the south. This quake hit in the early morning and knocked people and animals to the ground.

An officer at the Fort, writing about the quake, said there were two hard shocks lasting about 5 to 10 seconds each. Every pane of glass in windows at the Fort was broken, he said, but the frame wooden buildings did not suffer much damage.　　●

Oregon's Wonder Dog

Bobbie, Oregon Wonder Dog

Bobbie was a Collie dog that loved Silverton so much that he once walked 3,000 miles to get there.

Bobbie was owned by a family man in Silverton named Frank Brazier.

On Aug. 6, 1923, the Brazier family, as well as their pet dog, embarked on a sightseeing trip back east.

They traveled by automobile and all went well until they came to a small town by the name of Wolcott, Ind. There, somehow, Bobbie became separated from the Braziers and in the end they left without him.

According to witnesses who later stepped forward to verify the story, Bobbie started traveling in circles. Each circle became wider and wider until at last the dog had its bearings and struck due west.

Sometimes Bobbie walked along the shoulder of the road. Sometimes he cut across open fields. Every step he took was one closer to his Silverton home.

Days and nights turned to months before a woman in The Dalles took in the skeleton of a dog.

"His feet were cut and bleeding so badly I don't know how there could be any blood left in his body," she said.

Until there was some meat on his bones, Bobbie rested up at the house in The Dalles. The woman heard him the morning he left.

"He barked once to say thanks and was gone," she said.

Bobbie trotted down the gorge and into Portland

before swinging south through the valley.

Frank Brazier had long before given up hope of seeing Bobbie again. But six months to the day he became lost, Bobbie came home.

Out of the clear blue, Bobbie exploded through the window of Frank Brazier's bedroom and started licking his master all over the face.

Word of the amazing dog that had come 3,000 miles was around Silverton by dark and the Willamette Valley by noon the next day.

Newspapers played up the story and they renamed Bobbie "Wonder Dog."

"Wonder Dog" became a hysteria, and more or less to appease his fans, he was exhibited in Portland. After the first day it was estimated that 50,000 persons had touched and petted the famous dog.

Too much of a good thing wasn't much fun for Bobbie. He was bruised beyond endurance. The second day a woven wire barricade enclosed him.

It took years for the fame to subside. To this day Bobbie has received more fan mail than anyone else in Silverton, addressed simply to "Wonder Dog, Silverton, Oregon."

Salted Mine Swindles Investors

Around 1900, a gold mine was created in Oregon where geologists say there was no gold.

It was a bold stock-selling deal that evidently put considerable cash in the pockets of promoters and left many investors sadder, poorer and wiser.

In the mountains south of Joseph in the high Wallowa Mountains, a likely location for a mine was found. It was a lovely little valley and soon tunnels were dug, a camp set up and a lot of heavy equipment was moved to the site at about the 800-foot level.

There was a lot of publicity that claimed that high quantities of gold would soon be going through the stamp mill from "The Tenderfoot Mining and Milling Company," an outfit incorporated under the laws of South Dakota.

Stock was sold for $1 a share and many persons in the Northwest bought from 500 to 1,000 shares in the hope they would be "in on" the bonanza.

The sale went especially well in the East, and in about 1902 some of these Eastern investors decided to visit the mine. The mine was secretly "salted" before their arrival, according to reports, and the Tenderfoot Company also took another precaution. A supply of whiskey was hauled to the mine on two pack horses.

When the investors reached the mine after a weary horseback trip from the nearest town, they were given a hearty meal and served generous amounts of good whiskey.

It is said that when they had eaten and drunk

enough, they were escorted to the mine, and were wholly satisfied with what they saw — or were able to see. They left happily and never raised questions about the operation.

History is vague about the final demise of the gold mine that never had any gold, except what was carried in. In later years, some of the sheepish investors admitted that they never got one cent of their investment back, and the fellow who had been hired to pack in the whiskey recounted the tale of the operation with a chuckle.

All that remains to remind us of the gold mine is the name given to the valley — "Tenderfoot Basin" — and it is reached by "Tenderfoot Trail." ●

Oregon Water Once World Famous

Today, a popular soda water from France is shipped into Oregon and sold, but back in the early 1900s, Oregon produced a bottled mineral water that was made into pop and sold throughout the United States. And it was even shipped to Europe!

It was Calapooya Water from springs on the Upper Coast Fork of the Willamette River, at a little town called London, where there was a huge bottling works as well as the fancy Calapooya Springs Hotel and Health Resort.

Calapooya Water, as well as soda pop and salts, were bottled. They were labeled with a yellow, red

and blue sticker showing and Indian in full regalia. Across his middle were large latters, "Cal-A-Poo-Ya."

Gold Medal Winner

The water itself won a gold medal at the Alaska Yukon Exposition in Seattle in 1907, but efforts of London Springs, Inc., failed to keep the enterprise solvent.

For many years, however, the Calapooya Springs Hotel was an elegant and popular spot where people went for their health as well as for recreation.

It had a large swimming pool, park-like picnic grounds, and wide porches and balconies where guests could watch the activites and the sunsets. During Fourth of July celebrations, thousands came to the Wild West rodeos, races and fireworks, or gathered around the bandstand to listen to speakers or to music.

Today, few people remain who remember the hey-day of the resort and the boom town of London. The hotel was razed, the post office discontinued, the store burned, and the bottling works disappeared. ●

Flood of '61 Brings Bonanza

It's an ill flood that carries no good!

The flood of 1861 which swept down the Willamette and innundated the many homes and settlements of white people proved to be a bonanza for the Indians along the lower Columbia.

Never had they dreamed of such riches!

Rain and melting snow swelled the tributaries of the Willamette and its waters rose to unprecedented heights. Linn City, opposite Oregon City, was swept away, and flour mills, sawmills, warehouses, stores

and homes along the length of the river went floating towards the sea.

The Columbia River at Cathlamet and beyond was covered for days with lumber, flour, furniture and property of all kinds and the tides there made salvage easy.

Every Indian for miles around turned out and was hauling things as fast as he could. Every canoe was pressed into service. Some Indians, lacking a canoe, paddled logs out into the river to tow especially good prizes to shore. Indian children lined the banks, salvaging everything they could reach and whooping joyfully.

Flour was especially prized after it was found that the sacks were wet only about half an inch, and the inside flour was still dry and good. Later, much of the flour was traded for whiskey. The parties lasted for weeks.

One Indian thought he had found a valuable bounty when he spotted two white boxes floating by. He quickly hauled them into his canoe, but was observed jumping overboard shortly afterwards. He had rescued two hives of bees.

The flood was a sad affair for the whites who had built too close to the river, and who saw all their possessions washed away. But it made a lot of Indians happy — and richer, too. ●

In 1937, when secret service men caught a prominent Oregon mountaineer in President Franklin D. Roosevelt's room at Timberline Lodge unscrewing the toilet seat, they threatened arrest.

What did the fellow think he was doing? they asked.

When the mountaineer replied that he wanted to frame the President's photo to commemorate his 1937 visit to Oregon, the stern secret service fellows couldn't resist a laugh.

They decided to forego any legal action, since it might cause bad publicity for the President who already wasn't too popular among many of the influential citizens of the Northwest.

New Northwest discovery proving man lived in area 12,000 years ago excites scientists!

N.W. Hunters of 12,000 Years Ago

New evidence indicates that man has roamed and lived in the Pacific Northwest for over 12,000 years.

Not only were humans here, but these early residents hunted elephants in the valleys; they camped alongside the lakes and left tell-tale evidence of their lives, according to Washington State University scientists.

Discovery of mastodon bones near Sequim, Washington, on the Olympic Peninsula, with a spearpoint imbedded in a rib bone has given "the earliest evidence of man in the Pacific Northwest and the first certain evidence in all of North America that man hunted and butchered mastodons, a primitive form of elephant now extinct," says Carl E. Gustafson, Ph.D., one of the WSU investigators at the Sequim site.

The scientists, carefully excavating at Sequim, have also discovered charcoal firepits at different levels, indicating that man lived here over a time span of thousands of years. The shallowest charcoal pit has been carbon dated at 3,000 years; a lower pit proved to be over 6,000 years old, and a third and deeper pit awaits dating. Dr. Gustafson suspects that it may have been used by the early mastodon hunters.

Many other interesting things have been unearthed in connection with the Sequim dig. Between the layers of earth covering the different levels of fire-pits is a one- to two-inch layer of ashes which has been identified as coming from fallout of Mt.

Mazama's eruption (Crater Lake in Oregon).

Paleontologits who have come to the site to collect pollen and seeds from the deposits at the time the mastodon died have determined that the area was dominated by a tundralike environment, dotted with patches of willows and shrubs. Cattails were abundant, along with grasses and sedges.

A Sequim rancher, Emanuel Manis, made the discovery of the mastodon site when he started to dig a duck pond in his front pasture in 1977. His backhoe unearthed what he thought at first was a curved and polished piece of wood about four feet long.

A few seconds later, he brought up a second piece, almost eight feet long. These were tusks, but Manis did not suspect then that they would bring dramatic new knowledge about the life of early man in the Northwest!

Washington State University archaeologists, notified of the tusk find, were on the site about a week later. Discovery of the rib fragment with the spearpoint was made by Dr. Gustafson. Then a mastodon molar was found, and the scientists knew they were in luck.

The discoveries were so significant that the National Science Foundation immediately granted emergency funds so excavations could continue while long-term funding was being arranged.

Further analysis showed that the mastodon with the spear in its rib had been alive at the time of injury and probably lived for several months after being wounded because there were signs of bone healing around the spearpoint.

From cuts and scratches on the mastodon's other bones, Dr. Gustafson speculates that the hunters may have come upon the mastodon at a waterhole and killed it; or they may have discovered a fresh carcass and butchered it.

"Obviously the embedded spearpoint was not from an immediately fatal thrust, else there would not be any healing," Dr. Gustafson says.

The scientists expect the excavations to continue for several years while they continue to look for new clues about the people who lived here 12,000 years ago.

Other evidence that man existed in the Southwest United States about the same time has been found in California. It would seem to follow that he probably roamed the entire West Coast from California to the tip of the Olympic Peninsula and was also present in Oregon.

However, except for the sandals found in a cave near Ft. Rock in Eastern Oregon, no other evidence of man's presence this long ago has been found here as yet. The Ft. Rock sandals are said to date back to about 13,000 years ago, but some scientists are questioning the correctness of this date.

Dr. C.M. Eikens of the department of archaeology at the University of Oregon says the Willamette Valley has yielded evidence of man's presence here 5,000 to 6,000 years ago, but he points out that the valley has "filled up" with sediments, and this has probably buried any earlier evidence so deep it may never be found.

The Manis Archaeological Site at Sequim is open to the public and visitors are welcome. Excavations are discontinued during late fall and winter, and begin again in the spring. During this period, visits can be arranged by appointment only. A small admission fee helps offset the Manises' cost of keeping the site open for public education and enjoyment. ●

Oregon Historical Society Photo

When auto made its debut in Oregon it was not popular with many of the 'horse and buggy' class. They said noise frightened horses. This unpopularity made it very difficult for auto owners to get funds appropriated for road improvements to keep their cars from miring in mud.

Oregon Visitors Often Mired in Mud

The first oiled road in the United States was probably the one joining Portland with Linnton. It was oiled by the newly formed Portland Automobile Club, after Multnomah County Commissioners refused to oil the road on the grounds that the cost was too great for the value received. After all, not everyone had cars in 1905 and were interested in road conditions.

The Portland Automobile Club was organized primarily for the purpose of developing better roads upon which to operate automobiles, and the new club lost no time in getting started on its main project. After the commission turned down the oiling project, the AAA's Road Committee decided to oil the road themselves, and raised the money to do it.

During their first year, 1905, the club also succeedded in establishing a ferry across the river at St. Johns and improved St. Johns Boulevard to make it possible to have a circle drive of the city of Portland. Members turned out with pick and shovels on "road work days."

In words of an early club president, improvements were needed to get Portland "out of the mud." W.J. Clemens also cited work on the Rex Hill, south of Tigardville (now Tigard), which was notoriously bad, as needed "to give Portland an opening into the Willamette Valley and to allow tourists from California and Southern Oregon to come to Portland without being mired."

Another early road project of the Club was the development of the Mt. Hood road and much of the work on this project was under the direction of Henry Wemme, who eventually bought the old Barlow toll road section around Mt. Hood and gave it to the state to be operated as a toll-free road. The Club budgeted funds for improvement work on this road for several years, culminating in 1911 when they raised $50,000 for the project. ●

Horse Pulled Streetcars Lost Shirt

The last remaining Portland horse-drawn streetcar sits on a corner at 3737 SE Adams Street in Milwaukie, Oregon, at the site of the Milwaukie Historical Society Museum.

So small that it almost looks like a toy, the little streetcar was in operation from about 1872 to 1893 on the streets of Portland and up and down its hills.

It was drawn by one horse, except on the steepest hill, when a "hill horse" was added to help pull the

load. It is reported that then, as in later years, the public transportation system was not a very profitable operation, and one company after another "went broke" with their horse-operated businesses.

However, the surviving streetcar is in fine condition today, having been restored from a dilapidated state by a man named Damon Trout of North Plains, who owned it at one time and later donated it to the museum.

The Historical Society building, next door to the streetcar, is also of great historical interest. It is the old George Wise farmhouse which dates back to 1865. It was originally located at "Lakewood" and was moved to its present site and restored by concerned community effort in June, 1975. The farmhouse was given to the Society by United Grocers with the stipulation that it be moved from the company's property.

According to Museum Curator Chris McDonald, the moving and restoration could never have been accomplished without the help of the many individuals and groups who rallied around to assist. These included high school students, telephone company volunteers, the Marine Reserves, members of the Fire Department and many others.

The museum, open Saturdays and Sundays from 11 a.m. until 3 p.m., is also open for guided tours for groups or individuals by appointment. To make arrangements call Mrs. McDonald at 659-2998. ●

Dog Hero of Indian War

A shepherd dog was the hero of Happy Canyon in Eastern Oregon during the Indian War of 1878.

When sheepherders in the mountains were warned that the Indians were on the warpath and were killing everyone they caught, they abandoned their sheep and left the hills on their horses in great haste to reach their families and get to a safe place.

Jerry, a dog belonging to Jeremiah Barnhart, was left behind in the mountains with the sheep and he kept faithful watch over the large bands. When the sheepherders returned to check their losses, they found Jerry in command, with no sheep missing.

But a large number of sheep from other flocks had been added and had to be returned to their rightful owners.

Eliza R. Barchus

Famed "Mt. Hood Artist" was mother

By MARCIA PRY

Eleanor Roosevelt wrote about her; the State of Oregon adopted a resolution honoring her; she won a gold medal at the Lewis & Clark Exposition in 1905, and people say of her, "God made Mt. Hood, but Eliza Barchus made Mt. Hood famous."

Eliza R. Barchus, the Oregon artist, and her paintings are enjoying a revival both because of the inherent appeal of the art work and because one of her children, Agnes Barchus, wrote a book about her, "Eliza R. Barchus, the Oregon Artist."

The artist began her painting career in 1884 and continued portraying Oregon and other natural scenes of beauty well into this century.

Evelyn Greenstreet, in her foreward to the book, commented that Mrs. Barchus quite literally "raised her children with a paintbrush," especially after the death of her husband. Now many of Mrs. Barchus' paintings, some of which were traded for services to help her family, are again gaining popularity.

"I remember when I was about five or six years old," wrote Miss Barchus, "what wonderful fun it was to watch Mama cut a roll of canvas. She would unroll part of it and let it lie flat on the floor, then would draw the outlines of the sizes she needed, and then, to my way of thinking, the fun would begin.

"She would use scissors for the first two or three cuts, then let the scissors 'scoot' along with the grain of the canvas. To me it was such a wonderful sound

—51—

that I would laugh so hard I could hardly stop."

But cutting and stretching the canvas was only a small part of the work for Mrs. Barchus. Her lifespan alone would allow her some recognition; she died Dec. 31, 1959, just a few weeks after celebrating her 102nd birthday. And for those who knew her, her spirit and energy were remarkable qualities. But for most, it is her paintings that have created for her a place in history.

In the artist's own words: "I painted and sold hundreds of oil paintings of Mt. Hood, Mt. Shasta, the Three Sisters, Crater Lake, Multnomah Falls and Mt. Rainier, as well as the beauty spots of Alaska, the Yellowstone, the Yosemite and other scenes in the West. But somehow or other the business instinct does not seem to go with the artistic instinct, and while I had the joy of creation, those who have handled my work have usually made most of the money. I presume I have painted several thousand pictures of Mt. Hood and of other beauty spots of Oregon, so I have done my part to advertise Oregon and bring tourists here to see the originals of my paintings."

Her many paintings of Oregon's beautiful Mt. Hood earned for her the title of "Mt. Hood Artist." And her paintings earned for her many honors. In 1905, Mrs. Barchus was awarded a gold medal from the Lewis & Clark Centennial Exposition and World's Fair "for the finest collection of oil paintings of Northwest Scenery."

In 1957, as Eliza Barchus celebrated her 100th birthday, Eleanor Roosevelt paid the artist homage by writing of her, "In those days, becoming a career woman was fraught with many disadvantages and hardships, and becoming a nationally known famous artist, without the present-day help afforded by art societies and art museums, was a rare achievement.

Besides raising her family, painting and selling her own pictures, she instructed others, some of her students going on to make names for themselves in the art world.''

Miss Barchus, the daughter, when in her 80s, recalled experiences of growing up with an artist mother who was also a traveler, a barterer, a gardener, a writer of songs and poems, and, indicental to everything lse, a woman who lived to be more than 100 years old.

At various times when the artist received publicity for herself or her paintings, the family would receive letters from people throughout the United States who owned a Barchus painting or took painting lessons from Mrs. Barchus or remembered her booth at the Lewis & Clark Exposition.

Paintings were created to trade for construction of her house, for travel expenses, for medical and dental services, for many things Mrs. Barchus lacked either the time or money to provide for her family. There must be many Barchus paintings around, and even more abound in a style similar to hers.

On her style and signature her daughter points out, ''Eliza Barchus signed all of her paintings BARCHUS. Occasionally one shows up similar to her style, but not signed. Such are paintings of some of her art pupils, and are not genuine Barchus paintings. They may have a few of her brush strokes on them, however. She gave paintings to a large number of art students before and around the turn of the century, and even in 1913 when she made a special trip to Skagway, Alaska, and organized a painting class.

''At first 'the Oregon Artist' dated all of her paintings, but she soon learned that her customers preferred the older ones; and thinking she would not have a ready sale for her latest ones, she discontinued the practice of dating them.''

In addition to her paintings, her postcards, which first came out in 1906, also became popular and sought-after items. They were among the first postcards in color to be introduced in the West and were sold as inexpensive souvenirs of her paintings.

The cards had scenes of Mt. Hood and Mt. Rainier in the regular size and the same two scenes and Crater Lake in the giant size. Later, a sepiatone Timberline card with a poem was published.

The artist gave many of these postcards to servicemen during World War II, and they have since become treasured family mementoes. ●

"Lady" Sold at Auction

From the Portland Daily Bee
March 27, 1877

American papers have often commented upon the fact that in some parts of England, women have been sold at public auction during the last month. Yesterday the novel sight of a woman being sold under the hammer was witnessed by hundreds of people in front of Curris's auction store.

When it became known that such a sale was to be made, a large crowd gathered to see the woman, and many were wondering if the authorities would allow such a disgraceful scene to go on. At 10:30 the woman was brought out.

Her name was unknown, but she was recognized by some of the bystanders as a person who had worked in a millinery establishment before the fire, and her character had never been questioned. She seemed perfectly composed in the presence of so large a crowd, and never moved a muscle of her face as the auctioneer called out for the first bid.

She stood in an elevated position, dressed in plain muslin, without any special attempt at display. She was a handsome brunette, with regular features, dark hair and eyes, and a complexion as pure as wax. She was finally knocked down to $8 and to the surprise of everybody, the bidder was a married man.

He says the woman is somewhat dilapidated, but he thinks he can melt down the wax and make her into candles for Christmas trees. She originally cost $800 in New York, the workmanship being of the best, and was for a long time displayed in a Broadway milliner's window before she was shipped to the Comstock. ●

ABRAHAM LINCOLN

Gov. Lincoln of Oregon?

If Abraham Lincoln had accepted the governorship of Oregon when it was offered to him in 1849, would history have been altered?

If Lincoln had come west to the new territory as its governor, would he have returned to the East to become President of the United States 11 years later?

And would this great man subsequently have met his destiny and been downed by the assassin's bullet, or would he, like many others who came to Oregon, have decided to live out his years more obscurely right here on the beautiful West Coast?

At the time that President Zachary Taylor sent word to Lincoln that he could have the governorship of the Oregon Territorial government by presidential appointment, the land which is now Oregon was still being settled by pioneers who made the long, hard and dangerous trek across-country by wagon train. Indians were still a threat in many areas, and life in the new territory was hard.

The territorial government of Oregon had been created by the legislature on August 13, 1848, only a year before. The first territorial governor of Oregon was Joseph Lane, who was appointed by President James Polk. Lane resigned after Taylor was elected president.

Previous to the creation of the Oregon Territorial Government, there had been no real government here, only that organized by the settlers as a provisional government while the area was still under a "joint occupancy" agreement with Great Britain.

This agreement was made in 1818 and lasted for 30 years.

Some history books say Lincoln declined the governorship of Oregon on account of the objections of his wife. Evidently the hardships of life on the Western frontier did not appeal to her.

In any case, Lincoln did not come to Oregon, and he went on to be elected President of the United States in 1860. He freed the slaves and made history as leader of the Union during the Civil War and was subsequently asassinated in 1865.

A copy of the letter written by Lincoln declining the appointment as Oregon Territory governor was reprinted in the Oregonian on October 6, 1885. It gave no reason for his refusal of the position.

The Oregonian also reported that Lincoln had previously declined the secretaryship of the Oregon Territory. The appointments, according to historians, were offered because "Mr. Lincoln expected a valuable place," for past favors in behalf of President Taylor. When the only ones offered were ones which he could or would not accept, he did not complain, and asked nothing else, according to the historian.

In 1886, the Oregonian printed another story about Lincoln which contended that Oregon played a significant role in Lincoln's election as President in 1860.

"It is altogether within probability that it was the vote of Oregon in Horace Greeley's hands that made Lincoln's nomination possible," the paper said. If Oregon's five votes had been cast for William H. Seward, instead of for Edward Bates, of Missouri, Seward would have been eight and a half votes ahead of Lincoln on the second ballot, instead of only three and a half votes ahead, and Lincoln might not have been able to take the lead on the next ballot. On the third ballot, Oregon gave Lincoln its five votes, to help him win. The total number of voters in Oregon in 1860 was 14,410.

During the Civil War years, Oregon barely missed joining the Confederacy. Oregon Senator Joseph Lane was pro-slavery and believed that the election of Lincoln was an attack on the constitutional rights of the South. He thought the slavery states had a right to withdraw from the Union and pledged himself to assist them. (Lane was a former governor of Oregon and had been a well-known Indian fighter.) He led the disunion party in the United States Senate at the outbreak of the Civil War.

Governor John Whiteaker, who was governor of Oregon in 1861 when the war broke out, was also a believer in both state supremacy and what he termed the "divine right of slavery." In a speech delivered to the people of Oregon in May, 1861, he declared President Lincoln would get no troops from Oregon to aid in carrying on the "wicked and unnatural war upon the South."

The Oregonian in 1868 tells how the election of a legislature that was anti-slavery in 1862 kept Oregon from supporting Governor Whiteaker's stand and probably kept the state from joining the Confederacy.

Elizabeth Scott Duniway was 78-years-old and had spent most of her adult life working for women's suffrage in Oregon before she saw women get the vote. Governor Oswald West asked her to sign state's Suffrage Proclamation.

N.W. Women: "Half Dolls, Half Drudges and All Fools,"

By Jean Ward

Nineteenth Century women of the West are often ignored by authors of American history textbooks and are treated as stereotyped pioneer stock who, with a "feminine touch," helped bring civilization to the wilderness. In contrast, revered names of women of the East — Susan B. Anthony, Carrie Chapman Catt, Elizabeth Cady Stanton — are familiar to students of American history. But who were the women of the West who left us a valuable legacy?

One name from the West which belongs on the roll of 19th Century women of accomplishment is Abigail Jane Scott Duniway. Portlanders can look to Duniway Park, Duniway School and the profile of Abigail Duniway on the John's Landing Tower as reminders of this remarkable woman, but these landmarks tell little of her special story.

In 1852, Abigail's parents and their nine children left Tazewell County, Ill., to travel to Lafayette, Ore. Despite a limited formal education of about five months, 17-year-old Abigail was given the task of keeping an overland diary in which she faithfully recorded events of the six-month journey.

Land fever prompted the great migration of 1852 as wagon trains rolled westward to realize settlers' dreams of rich acres under the Donation Land Law. But another fever, the plague of cholera, left its mark on many families who made the trip.

On June 20th, Abigail wrote of her frail mother, weakened by bearing 12 children, the deaths of three infant sons, the hardships of the journey, and the dreaded cholera: "Her wearied spirit took its flight and then we realized that we were bereaved indeed."

With pathos she recorded the Aug. 28 death of her three-year-old brother, Willie: "The ruthless monster death, not yet content, has once more entered our fold and taken in his icy grip the treasure of our hearts."

The sorrow of her mother's life and death stimulated Abigail to question the place of woman in what appeared to be a man's world. She recalled the agonized words of her mother when another daughter was born: "Poor baby! She'll be a woman some day. Poor baby! A woman's lot is so hard."

At the same time, Abigail's intelligence, ambition and independent spirit convinced her that women could be more than bearers of children and household "drudges." The circumstances of her marriage put this belief to the test.

Within a year of her arrival in Oregon, Abigail left a teaching job in Eola to marry Benjamin C. Duniway and join him on his donation land-grant farm. Characteristic of her independent spirit was her insistence that the word "obey" be deleted from the marriage vows.

Between 1853 and 1862 she performed the endless chores oa a farmer's wife and mother of four children, but somehow she found time to read and write. Uncertain of the wisdom of submitting early writing under her own name, she sent unsigned poetry to the Oregon City Argus and signed her work for The Oregon Farmer as "a farmer's wife." In 1859, at the age of 25, she published, under her own name, "Captain Gray's Company," a story of western migration.

Two events in 1862 were significant in shaping Abigail's future. The Duniway farm was lost when a great flood swept away the harvest and promissory notes could not be paid. After the family moved to Lafayette, Ben was permanently injured in a runaway horse accident. The resourceful Abigail became breadwinner as well as homemaker. In Lafayette, and later in Albany, she opened a private school and took in boarders, rising at three in the summer and four in the winter to care for her household before the day of teaching.

Married women in Oregon did not have rights to their own businesses until the Legislature adopted a Married Woman's Property Bill in 1874. However, in 1865, the persuasive Abigail enlisted financial assistance from wealthy Portland wholesaler Jacob Mayer to open a millinery business in Albany.

As a businesswoman, she observed women from all walks of life who had no financial independence and she remarked, "half of us are dolls, half of us are drudges, and all of us are fools." It was Ben who convinced her that conditions would never improve for women until they had the right to vote.

Believing in the woman's suffrage cause and impressed with the power of the printed word, Abigail established a newspaper, The New Northwest. Her 1871 advance for the paper read:

"We have served a regular apprenticeship at working — washing, scrubbing, patching, darning, ironing, plain sewing, raising babies, milking, churning and poultry raising. We have kept boarders, taught school, taught music, written for newspapers, made speeches and carried on an extensive millinery and dressmaking business . . . having reached the age of 36, and having brought up a family of boys to set type, and a daughter to run the millinery store, we proposed to edit and publish a newspaper; and we intend to establish it as one of the permanent institutions of the country."

Her paper could hardly compete with The

Oregonian which was edited by her brother, Harvey Scott, but she did not hesitate to refute his statement: "I am a foe to irresponsible voting, and giving women the right to vote would surely compound a felony."

Abigail's apprenticeship in public speaking was served the same year she started The New Northwest. In 1871 she managed Susan B. Anthony's two-month speaking tour of Oregon and Washington. The two women traveled by stage and steamer to speak wherever local officials would permit them to collect an audience.

While some of society criticized Abigail for "unwomanly" thoughts and behavior, she never lacked for speaking invitations. One lecture brochure listed such varied titles as "Constitutional Liberty," "The Temperance Problem and How to Solve It," "Courtship, Marriage and Divorce," "Why Women Are Sick," and "Cooperative Housekeeping." A Portland newspaper described her talents as lecturer-writer:

"As an extemporaneous speaker she is logical, sarcastic, witty, poetic and often truly eloquent. As a critic she is merciless, as an enemy forgiving; and after having her 'say,' conciliatory. As a writer she is forceful, argumentative and sometimes voluminous, but it hardly necessary to add, never dull."

Abigail believed in what she called the "still hunt" approach to woman's suffrage. She did not believe in threatening men, for she realized that men alone had the power to grant women the right to vote. She was in conflict with prohibitionists who sought to link suffrage with their cause.

Women's suffrage was defeated five times in Oregon before victory in 1912. No other state had to wage six campaigns to achieve the vote for women. Abigail's role in bringing the vote to over 75,000 women in Oregon was recognized when Gov. Oswald West asked her to write Oregon's Woman Suffrage Proclamation. At the age of 78 she could reflect on earlier successes in Washington and Idaho and her 40 years of struggle in Oregon.

In 1914, one year before her death, Abigail Duniway published her autobiography "Path Breaking: An Autobiographical History of the Equal Suffrage Movement in Pacific Coast States." The closing lines of the mother of equal suffrage in Oregon are timeless:

" . . . women of today, free to study, to speak, to write, to choose their occupation, should remember that every inch of this freedom was bought for them at a great price. It is for them to show their gratitude by helping onward the reforms of their own time, by spreading the light of freedom and truth still wider. The debt that each generation owes to the past it must pay to the future." ●

– Sketch Courtesy of Oregon Historical Society
(By Dean Collins, used in "Stars of Oregon")

Romance of Beaver

It's appropriate that the S.S. Beaver, the first steamship to round Cape Horn, came to the North American continent at the mouth of the Columbia River, then ran aground in Oregon, the "Beaver State" — but it happened long before there was any state, in a time when there were more beavers than people in the land.

Indeed, the vessel was named by the famous Hudson's Bay Company for the fur bearing animal which was one of the staples of its early Northwest trade. Built in Blackwall, England, in 1834-35, the "steam brigantine" was 101 feet long, 20 feet wide inside the paddle boxes, 33 feet wide outside, with 11½ feet of draft.

And her claim to being the first steamship to round the cape is perhaps a little tenuous, because her voyage from the shipyard to the Hudson's Bay outpost at Fort Vancouver, up the Columbia River, was under sail. The two side paddle wheels, each 13 feet in diameter and five feet wide, were not in position during the voyage, and were installed permanently only after arrival at her destination.

She sailed for the New World under the command of Capt. David Home and with a crew of 26 men on August 29, 1835. She was accompanied on her maiden voyage by the bark Columbia as consort, but the Beaver was much faster and often had to shorten sail in order not to get too far ahead of the Columbia.

To the land-lubber, it may seem incongruous that

after rounding Cape Horn, the two ships headed for Hawaii — but sailors know that is the route of the tradewinds. They reached Robinson Crusoe Island in December, staying five days to replenish their water supplies, then reached Honolulu on February 4, 1836, remaining there for 22 days as they took on stores.

Their North American landfall was Cape Disappointment, on the Washington side of the mouth of the Columbia River, and they sailed into Baker's Bay just east of the cape on March 19 to take on a Hudson's Bay pilot, Mr. Latta. He was successful on April 4 in guiding the Beaver across the bar, only to get stuck in the sand of Tongue Point. This occasioned only a brief delay, however, and on April 10, after a passage of 226 days from England, the Beaver reached Fort Vancouver.

After the paddle wheels were installed, the pioneer steamship became an excursion boat. Parties from Fort Vancouver were taken "up to the (Hudson's Bay Company) sawmill" — about five miles up the Columbia from the fort — "and back to the lower part of Menzie's Island." The excursions also extended into present-day Oregon, the trip being made from "Fort Vancouver to the mouth of the Willamette River, from thence around Wapatoo (Sauvie's) Island by way of the Willamette Slough" — now called the Multnomah Channel — "to the Columbia and then up that river to the place of starting."

After the trip, all hands were piped on deck to "splice the main braces" — a euphemism for a drink of grog. After two months of junketing, the Beaver sailed for Puget Sound as a trading vessel for Hudson's Bay Company.

Although much of that period in the Beaver's history was spent in voyages between Alaska and

Puget Sound, she occasionally braved the high seas of the Pacific in coastal trade. Indeed, she once got herself arrested at the newly-created American custom house at Astoria for clearing without proper papers.

For 52 years the Beaver plied the waters of the North Pacific, Puget Sound and the Straits of Georgia, for many of those years in the fur trade for Hudson's Bay Company between Alaska and the Sound. She was overhauled in 1860 and equipped with staterooms to carry passengers between Victoria and New Westminster.

Although the Beaver, like most cargo ships built in those days, was equipped with armament at the shipyard — five nine-pounder guns — in early years were in peaceful trade. In 1862, however, she was chartered to the Royal Navy and designated HMS Beaver, being used as a floating magazine. Yet the British Admiralty advanced 500 pounds sterling, less than the charter price, and the difference was made up by the colony of British Columbia, still a Hudson's Bay Company fief.

After a brief episode as a warship, however, the Beaver was placed in a more harmonious service, conducting the hydrographic survey of British Columbia waters. Her master, Lt. Cm. Lawrence Farrington, RCN, called her work varied and free of red tape, checking and reporting on the condition of upper Vancouver Island settlements, carrying out some land surveys, doing some police work.

Even though the Beaver's history records few events of dramatic moment, she is remembered with interest and affection by maritime buffs. "She was built in the most substantial manner of live oak and greenheart, the timbers being held together by copper bolts'' — this an excerpt from the introduction in her log.

Her two engines and boilers were built in Birmingham by Boulton Watt & Company (the Watt in the firm a son of James Watt, inventor of the recycling steam engine) and were the old-fashioned side-lever type, with 35 horsepower each. They were always stopping on dead center, and being ponderous affairs, it required a small army of men to get them over and make them strike out for themselves. After they had been in use some 50 years, the engineers who understood that style of engine were nearly all dead, and it was with difficulty that men could be secured to handle them.

In the words of one of several fascinating accounts of the Beaver's life in the archives of the Oregon Historical Society, ''the Beaver came to her untimely end in July, 1888, after a career of extraordinary vicissitudes. After 52 years of continuous service in almost every capacity, she met the death worth so honest a ship, by running on the rocks of Burrard Inlet.

''There she hung, obstinately resisting all efforts to dislodge her, as if wearied of her toilsome life, and resenting the attempts to disturb her rest. For four years the stiff old hulk hung together, and then was purchased by a firm in Vancouver, who worked up her staunch timbers into souvenir canes and made medals of her copper and brasses, deriving a handsome profit from their sale.'' ●

Repaired and outfitted again in 1870, the Beaver became a nautical jack-of-all-trades, towing, freighting and carrying passengers.

—Photo Courtesy of Oregon Historical Society

Pete French — Hero or Villain?

By Morton Spence

"He had to be killed."

This after-the-fact judgment of a friend of Pete French appears to sum up the slaying of one of early Oregon's most colorful characters, a millionaire cattle king, on his "P" Ranch near the southeastern corner of the state.

It was the day after Christmas, 1897, Exactly what happened cannot be known for sure. It was reported by eyewitnesses that Pete French had dismounted from his horse to open a gate for a group of his cowhands — he called them "vaqueros," reflecting his heritage from the Spanish-influenced cattle country of California from whence he came — and Ed L. Oliver, a farmer, shot him in the back of the head.

Ed Oliver then got on his horse, apparently riding past the slain man's employees, some of them no doubt wearing six-shooters on their hips, and proceeded to his homestead. He later was arrested, tried for murder at Burns, the recently-established seat of Harney County, and acquitted — let off scot-free by a jury of his peers, fellow homesteaders all, not a cattleman among them.

It is said that Oliver later left the area where French had established his cattle empire, and located in Umatilla County.

As for Pete French, "He had to be killed."

The confusing circumstances leading to the murder of Pete French weren't sorted out, either in the official records of the time, or in later, often contradictory testimony of people who were at or near the scene. It seems to be true that no gun was on French's body. Some say he seldom was armed, although his cowboys often toted revolvers ("Protection against rattlesnakes, either reptiles or humans"); others reported that the tension between the cattle baron and the settlers had grown to the point that French surely had a gun on him.

The acquaintance who said his violent death was inevitable had a theory about what had happened. Maybe it isn't true, but it embellishes an already exciting story.

Rye Smith, of Happy Valley near the "P" Ranch, was the oldest contemporary of Pete French living in 1935 when he was quoted in the Oregonian as saying, "He always expected to be murdered."

Smith went on. "A great feller. Not afraid of nobuddy, or nothin'! Never saw such eyes — brilliant, wrap right around your head and tie knots behind! But they got him . . . guess somebody had to . . . I dunno . . . a pity!

"Anyway, a killer'd have to shoot him through the back of the head . . . couldn't nobody look in Pete's eyes and shoot him . . . generally went armed . . . quickest man on the draw ever in the country . . . but wasn't armed that day; leastways, they said he wasn't.

"But when they brought his body in, his coat was buttoned up crooked. Now, Pete French never in his life buttoned his own coat crooked. A smart dresser — always looked like a prince. My theory? Well, it looked to me like his vaqueros — they all loved him — kneeled beside him and pulled out his gun, on the idea it would go harder with his murderer to have shot an unarmed man . . . then bottoned his coat back crooked . . . I dunno. They'd do anything for Pete, worshiped him."

Then, the writer reports, the old man sighed

deeply. After all the years, the deed was still a sadness with him.

"But he had to be killed. I guess it was only a question of who'd have the honor — about everybody in them days wanted it."

Not everybody wanted Pete French dead, however, according to other testimony. A few years ago he was nominated by a committee of the Oregon Historical Society and then named to the Great Westerners Hall of Fame at the Western Heritage Center in Oklahoma City. The committee's report said Peter French was undoubtedly the Oregon cowman with the best known name; no other cattle raiser from the time the first cattle were brought up from California has received the attention given to French. His dramatic life and death are partly responsible.

But the spectacular events cannot erase the material accomplishments of Pete French when he was boss of the "P" Ranch, along the Donner and Blitzen Rivers in the shadow of the Steens Mountain.

French came to the Blitzen, a young man of 23, in the late spring of 1872 from California, where cattlemen were being made unwelcome by an influx of settlers — a movement of "progress" which two decades later would lead to violence and death in Oregon.

His sponsor and partner — and soon to be his father-in-law — was Dr. Hugh James Glenn, a wealthy wheat rancher in the Sacramento Valley. The young man found a settler named Porter who had a small herd of cattle and, not being enamored of the cattle business, wanted to sell out. French bought his cattle and his branding iron, then set out to make the "P" Ranch famous.

Plenty of Backing

With 1,200 head of pretty fair Shorthorn cattle he

brought with him from California and the almost unlimited financial backing of Dr. Glenn, the budding cattle baron began to acquire land using the various strategems of the day, and by the time he was killed at the age of 48 his holdings were reported to be somewhere between 100,000 and 200,000 acres — a discrepancy accounted for partly by the often informal survey methods of the times, and partly by the disputed claims of settlers who had moved inside the boundaries of the ''P'' Ranch.

The lands included the western slopes of the Steens Mountain, that 40-mile-long piece of up-turned original earth surface, the east face of which rises 5,000 feet precipitously from the floor of the Alvord Desert — a geological wonder, an escarpment reaching to 9,740 feet elevation. The grass-covered western side, drained by the Donner and Blitzen Rivers, provides terrain for grazing cattle and browsing game, and a loop road now reaches within a few feet of the summit.

French also bought out a man named A.H. Robie, whose brand was a diamond; the Diamond Ranch, just north of the Steens, became part of the great ''P'' Ranch property. The price paid, between $20,000 and $30,000, was a large sum for those days — and there was not a titled acre in the deal. The land was Robie's only by right of occupation.

The Diamond Ranch included a large chunk of so-called ''swamp land'' — land which at least seasonally was under water — and which with other adjoining real estate was made available by the government for settlement under the Swamp Act for $1 an acre. Pete French urged, or dispatched, or persuaded, or ordered his cowboys to homestead the swamp land, and then he bought it from them at most reasonable prices. Later, when other settlers moved in and challenged French's title to some of the lands, it was reported that cowboys from the "P" Ranch were sent out in a strange contrivance — a rowboat loaded on a wagon. They then were able to testify in court that they had traversed "every inch" of the contested acreage in a boat, "proof" that it was, indeed, "swamp land."

The empire comprised the holdings of the French-Glenn Company, and whatever the actual acreage, it was considerable. There was a difference, too, between the usual pattern of large cattle companies — including some others in eastern Oregon — and the way Peter French operated. Other cattlemen came to new country to "harvest the grass." French came to develop the country.

After taking up land and establishing the home ranch in the valley of the Blitzen River where it hits the flats, French ditched the marshes, drained the swamps, built barns and corrals and fenced with rock walls between the rimrocks, and with solid juniper posts — many of them still standing strong. He built a large house at the headquarters ranch, painted it white, and of course it was called the White House. The lumber was hauled from Canyon City on wagons with 10- and 12-mule teams.

The market for his cattle, and the source of most of the ranch's supplies, was 225 miles south at Winnemucca, Nev. He married Dr. Glenn's daughter; she refused to live at the remote "P" Ranch (she would have been the only woman in the desert vastness) and they later were divorced. Then Dr. Glenn was fatally shot by his bookkeeper, and the "P" Ranch holdings reverted entirely to Pete French.

In the meantime, around 1888, Ed Oliver and some other settlers had moved in, building fences around their places, sometimes right out in the middle of one ot Pete French's fields; fields on the "P" Ranch were measured by the square mile. "A surly fellow, that Oliver," one cattleman described him. He probably had enough to be surly about.

Well, Pete French wanted an uninvaded open range. The settler wanted a home. Oliver wouldn't go or be bought out. Pete wouldn't consent to his staying. It was a standoff that lasted about nine years.

None of the disputes or difficulties deterred the ever-hopeful homesteaders. Covered wagons creaked and lumbered down hillsides and across the open country, bringing in families, mothers looking out and wondering where they could "light" and start a home. There were rumors of railroads coming. Some claimed to be "in the know" — but nobody knew, and the tips were worthless. But the whisperings kept everyone uneasy.

Everyone, that is, but Pete French. He was too busy with fences, busy with cattle, and dogs, and horses. Busy with ditches and drainage, busy acquiring more land. He had brought in purebred Shorthorn bulls, and the quality of his herd was improving. In fact, the cattle king, the baron of the "P" Ranch, had worked hard for what he had. He was the boss, and his men were said to respect him. He was a leader whom men followed, and from his office in the White House he ruled what had become an empire.

But in the little farm houses, resentment ran high. French and a couple of other big operators, including John Devine of the Alvord Ranch on the other side of Steens Mountain, were seeking eviction notices against the settlers. Men tightened their belts, set their jaws grimly and prepared for war.

The gun, as they saw it, was the great equalizer.

Such was the atmosphere around Harney County. When Ed Oliver shot Pete French, the settlers felt their cause had been served righteously. At the trial in Burns, Oliver's lawyer pleaded self-defense, and testimony stated that French had quirted Oliver on five separate occasions. On the day of the shooting, it was alleged, French fired first, the bullet striking Oliver's hatband. Oliver had drawn his six-gun. He fired once. The bullet went through French's head.

Although there is not mystery about who killed Pete French, it remains a puzzle that Oliver was not gunned down by French's men, right then or later. In various accounts in the file at the Oregon Historical Society are statements such as these:

"Perhaps to no man has come the loyalty his men felt for Pete French. Find a man who worked on the 'P' Ranch in the old days — and they are almost all gone — and they invariably laud him to the skies . . .

"'He was always so pleasant; lived a wonderful life — couldn't live cooped up. That was the way to live; how puny all our lives seem today, compared with lives of those men . . . . Yes, Pete French was a better man than many give him credit for.'"

Yet the records allow him to remain an enigma — remaining aloof, a shadowy figure who had few really close friends. "French was a small man, his weight estimated at 125 pounds. He was dapper and dressy, not much of a mixer, did not drink or smoke, but indulged in the outmoded habit of chewing tobacco." One of his biographers, long-time Moro newspaper publisher Giles French (no relation), talked about the loyalty of Pete French's hired hands, but went on, "those who hated him did so with equal ardor."

Apparently Ed Oliver hated Pete French "with ardor." And there were enough others who shared his temper about the man that, in effect, the courts agreed: "He had to be killed." ●

What Wiped Out N.W. Natives?

What happened to the once populous and powerful Indian people that evidence indicates once lived in what is now Oregon and Washington State?

Were they wiped out by some mysterious disease? Or did some natural catastrophe destroy them?

No one knows for sure, but by the time Lewis and Clark made their western trip, there were relatively few Indians left.

Old Indian legends told to the earliest white settlers by aged Indians claimed they were once a powerful race, but had provoked Divine anger and been destroyed.

And this claim is probably true, although the manner of decimation is uncertain.

Ancient Indian campfires that stretched for long lines along beaches were found by early settlers. These had trees that were then more than 100 years old growing on top of them. Many stone hammers were found around each of these campfires. On a nearby mountain, extensive fortifications were found that would have required large armies to build and defend.

Another indication of a large population was the remains of a flint factory found at the Clackamas River and recorded in early records. Thousand of arrowheads have been found, and continue to be found, throughout the region, indicating many arrowmakers and many hunters.

Some historians say disease brought by the first visitors from Europe wiped out the Indian population that once filled Oregon and Washington from the Cascades to the Pacific Ocean. But there is much other evidence that the Indians were at the height of their power and prosperity much earlier, and that by the time the first white men came on ships the tribes were already moving towards extinction.

Some archeologists believe that the extinction of the large mammals, like the mammoth, can be attributed to overhunting by the large population of people that roamed the Western slopes.

The white men who came to the Pacific Coast brought smallpox and measles, and these took their toll of the Indians that were left, but there is evidence that some other, strange disease that history failed to give a name was the main cause of destruction of the extensive tribes. Some speculate that it was malaria, others suggest it may have been a deadly form of influenza.

There is some evidence that if it was disease that destroyed the Indians, it may have been brought here by the visitors from the Orient, or by plunderers from Spain, both of whom visited the West Coast of North America long before the recorded history of the area began. ●

Husband Caught After 25 Years

"No task is too great for a woman if she sets her mind to it," said Mrs. Gawley and to prove her point she went out and chased her runaway husband for 25 years, until she caught up with him in Oregon.

"We were married in 1873 in Ohio and for the first three years he practiced the sawmill filer trade," Mrs. Gawley said.

"We had three children, a boy and two girls, when he ran out on us.

"I could not support the family myself, so I decided to find my runaway husband and make him pay. One time I was close to finding him because he mailed

$400 to me.

"But I never could verify his whereabouts. I used the money to keep up my search.

"I went to Hoquiam, Wash., because I heard he was working there. He was not. The next word I heard was from his brother who had seen him in New Orleans. I could not find him there, either.

"I had offers of marriage during this time, but I refused. I had a fight to win and I couldn't win if I remarried.

"Finally, I got word to my husband, James, through a friend and it was arranged that he would join me in Detroit and we would take up life where we had left off. I went to Detroit. He did not.

"Everything went wrong. For a number of years I sewed, washed and did odd work to support the children. But by hard work and persistence I traced down a friend of James' in Michigan. He said my husband could be found in Oregon."

Mrs. Gawley confronted her husband on a downtown Portland street, not far from where he was living. She demanded that he make past restitutions and give her half interest in the property he owned.

It had taken Mrs. Gawley 25 years to locate her husband, and never had she considered giving up. By then her youngest child, a son, was 32 years old.

"During my years of searching, a great many changes have taken place," Mrs. Gawley said upon finding her husband.

"I have been too busy to grow old, but James, my husband, is aged and his body is hunched over. I'm afraid after all this, he might not be much good to me." ●

Oregon's One Big Splurge

One hundred years after Meriwether Lewis and William Clark were the first white men to journey from the Missouri River to the Pacific Coast, Oregon staged a summer-long spectacular "that let the rest of the country know that Oregon was here."

It was the "Lewis and Clark Exposition and Oriental Fair" and it covered 406 acres, cost $7 million, and was the first large exposition of international character ever held "in the far westerly

latitudes.''

The Exposition, which opened in the rain on June 1, 1905, covered the slopes and terraces overlooking Guilds Lake in what is now Northwest Portland in the vicinity of the old Montgomery Ward store.

Guilds Lake itself was an important part of the Fair, and it was dredged and filled with water pumped in from the Willamette River, then spanned by the "Bridge of Pleasure" which connected the main grounds to the peninsula. Beyond the bridge were a kite-shaped race track and a Wild West show, as well as a livestock display. The lake was also the scene of a dazzling water carnival, and was used for water sports, canoes, and gondolas. At night it reflected the twinkling of 90,000 lights.

The main entrance to the Exposition was near

Northwest 26th and Upshur in what was then called Willamette Heights. It was lined with Corinthian columns and flanked by spectacular buildings built especially for the occasion. The States Building, which housed exhibits for at least 18 other states, was the largest. The Forestry Building, the only building to survive on the site after the Fair, was the largest log building in the world. (It burned in the 1960's.) The Inn, built to house visitors, had 1,000 rooms.

The Fair was Oregon's first appearance in the spotlight, and the whole state loved it and profited by it. Later it was said that the Exposition started the ''biggest migration west since the covered wagon.''

More than 2.5 million persons visited the fair before it closed 137 days after President Theodore Roosevelt pressed a golden telegraph key in Washington, D.C., which opened the gates

The day the fair opened, it was $178,000 in debt, and the initial crowds were not spectacular. Fair officials, faced with $4,000 a day operating expenses, panicked and went to Exposition President Henry Good asking, ''What can we do?''

In reply, he said he had a suggestion to make.

''Wait until the rain stops,'' Good said. The sun began to shine on June 7, and the fair, like the roses which lined many Portland streets even then, bloomed and prospered. It ended with a profit of $175,616 in the bank.

A number of special events held in connection with the Lewis and Clark Exposition in 1905 attracted worldwide interest. A transcontinental auto race started in New York City when two 800 pound gasoline runabouts called "Old Scout" and "Old Steady" headed west for the fair. Old Scout got lost on the last leg of the journey and turned up in Salem before finding its way to Portland, and Old Steady never did get here.

Another startling feature was the flights of the one-man airship "City of Portland." With the world still amazed with the first flight of Wilbur and Orville Wright just 2 years earlier, fair officials expressed their interest in flying by sponsoring flights around the city by 18-year-old Lincoln Beachley, "Boy Aeronaut." His plane was built by two Albany youths, and "looked like a katydid on ice skates," according to reports. It actually was two gas bags driven by motor. (Ten years later, at the 1915 San Francisco Fair, Beachley crashed to his death in the craft.) ●

"Little Egypt" Pleases Men

No hamburgers were to be had at the Lewis and Clark Exposition in Portland in 1905, but some of the other diversions on "The Trail," which was the entertainment area, were talked about for years.

The Floradora girls, who daringly showed bare knees as they danced the "Hootchy-Kootchy," were a highlight of the Exposition.

"Little Egypt" was also a crowd pleaser, and "Fatima," a muscle dancer of repute, shocked the ladies and delighted masculine fair goers.

There were camel rides available on the "Streets of Cairo," and at the "Iggorote Village" headhunters imported from the Fiji Isles stared back at the crowds.

Women attending the fair mostly wore the costume of the day—shirtwaists and skirts that almost swept the ground, and big, big hats adorned with fruits and flowers, veilings, feathers and quills. Bowlers were stylish for the men, and no lady would dream of going to the fair without hat and gloves.

Besides the people, there were also other visitors reported at the Exposition—mosquitoes by the millions, attracted from the Columbia and Willamette River wetlands by the prospect of a free lunch, courtesy of the 2.5 million visitors who attended the fair during its 137 days. ●

Many goddesses were on display at 1905 Lewis & Clark Exposition in Portland. Did one of them find her way to a shady woodland shrine near Camas, Washington?

Where Is Northwest Forest Goddess?

What has happened to "Minerva of the Northwest Woods?" Could she possibly have been a displaced goddess from the 1905 Lewis and Clark Exposition?

In 1943, a life-size statue of Minerva in a glass case was discovered enshrined in the forest near Government Mineral Springs, north of Camas.

A report carried in a Portland paper at the time said Leslie Werschkul, a woman vacationing near the spot where a summer hotel had been destroyed by fire, saw the statue near a picnic area. She was described as a "graphically white female figure, housed in a shadow box with a rustic roof."

Inquiries did not shed much light on the origin of the statue, or how she got to such a remote place. Although she was dubbed "Minerva," the writer of the time said his research showed that the Roman Minerva was always dressed in a martial helmet and held a shield on one arm. This Minerva was hatless, and in her hand she held a wreath instead of a shield.

Although there were many heroic sized plaster casts of sculptures from the St. Louis Fair of 1904 donated to the Oregon fair, none of the pictures of these statues matched the Lady of Mystery seen in the Gifford Pinchot National Forest.

What has happened to her since 1943 is equally mysterious. Does she still sit in her remote shrine, now overgrown and lost to forest visitors, or was she removed to another location, or vandalized? Possibly only the trees in the forest know the answer.   ●

Expo Relics Disappear

Although the Lewis and Clark Exposition and Oriental Fair took place in Portland just 74 years ago, today little tangible evidence remains of the event that was "the most extravagant and consequential spectacle ever staged in Oregon."

Guilds Lake was filled in shortly after the fair closed with soil sluiced from the hills. Today it is an industrial area.

The Forestry Building, which was the only building left standing at the Exposition site, burned to the ground in the 1960s. An administration building, which stood near the entrance of the Exposition, was reported moved along the old Hillsboro-Oregon City Highway in 1907 to a site in West Linn where it was remodeled as a residence. The Masonic Building is reportedly still standing after being moved to a location on Northwest Northrup, and the Lincoln Building was moved to Ladds Colony on Southwest Jefferson.

The Cash Register Building was acquired by the Congregational Church and moved to North Richmond Avenue and Ivanhoe Streets in St. Johns. It subsequently has housed the YWCA, the Lutheran Church, and an American Legion Post.

The only statues that survived the Exposition can still be seen in Washington Park. They are "The Coming of the White Man" by Hermon Atkins MacNeil, and "Sacajawea, the Bird Woman" by Alice Cooper. Twenty tons of Oregon copper donated by Portland physician Dr. Henry Waldo's company went into the Sacajawea statue, along with $7,000 donated by Women of America as a gift to Oregon. When it was unveiled, two of the principal speakers were women suffragists Susan B. Anthony and Abigail Scott Duniway.

The many other statues displayed at the 1905 Exposition, including the famous one of "The Cowboys" seen on most picture postcards from the fair, were on loan from St. Louis (from its fair the year earlier) and were returned to St. Louis after the Oregon event. ●

Cowardly Council Evades Issue

With the gates of the "Lewis and Clark Exposition and Oriental Fair" scheduled to open in less than a week, Portland was in turmoil over demands by the Anti-Saloon League that Northwest Portland saloons close for the duration of the fair.

Five city council members failed to show at council meeting on the day a vote on the question was to be taken. The Mayor and the four council members on hand sent the police to look for the missing members, with orders "to haul them to the session by force if necessary."

The police came up empty-handed. The missing members were not to be found, they said. The mayor then labeled them "yellow bellies" and the Oregon Journal carried the banner headline, "Cowardly Councilmen Will Not Face Issue."

The police also had other problems, and reported on the eve of the fair that the city was swollen with burglars, pickpockets, confidence men and thugs. Police Chief Charles Hunt issued a warning to householders and fairgoers to "bar their doors to strangers; don't carry large sums of money, and to watch their watches when in crowds." ●

Early Cookbooks Told All

The young bride coming west in the early 1900's wouldn't think of making the trip without bringing one of the two important cookbooks of the day.

These cookbooks were not just cookbooks, they were the faithful guide for keeping house in the 1900's, and their thick pages went far beyond just giving recipes.

One was the Buckeye Cook Book, published in 1887, and the other was the White House Cook Book, which came out in 1909.

The Buckeye Cook Book was dedicated to "Plucky Housewives, who master their work instead of allowing it to master them." It had a section on care of babies, a medical section, a few chapters on laundry, a chapter on chemistry of food and a special section called "Kitchen Wrinkles," in addition to recipes of all kinds.

In the Kitchen Wrinkles, the housewife was advised that "tomatoes are nice with cream and sugar," and she was warned to always stir caramel with a wooden spoon. Coffee syrup, it said, good for taking along when traveling, could be made by boiling one-half pound of coffee in three pints of water until the liquid was reduced to one pint. Then the liquid should be drained off and boiled again, adding enough sugar to give it the consistency of syrup. This mixture could then be bottled and sealed until one wanted a cup of coffee. At that time, two teaspoons of the syrup was put in a cup and boiling water poured in, making a "delicious cup of coffee."

The White House Cook Book was authored by Hugo Ziemann, steward of the White House, and Mrs. F.L. Gillette, and among its many features, it offered portraits of all the ladies of the White House. Hugo, it said, had "conducted the celebrated Brunswick Cafe in New York, and had brought his culinary talents to the Hotel Richelieu in Chicago before going to the White House." The preface further guaranteed that every recipe offered had been "tried and tested."

In addition to the recipes, the White House Cook Book also billed itself as "A comprehensive cyclopedia of information for the home." This information included the following bits of advice:

To keep milk sweet for long periods, put a spoonful of grated horseradish in the panful of milk — it will keep sweet for days.

To take spots out of clothes to be washed, rub spots with yolk of egg before washing.

For troublesome ants, put a heavy chalk line around the sugar box.

To make tough meat tender, lay for a few minutes in a strong vinegar water.

Use salt on pineapples as an antidote for the acid in the rind that causes swollen mouth and sore lips, rinse well.

To remove ink, wine and fruit stains, saturate in tomato juice (also removes stain from hands.)

To prevent odor of boiling ham or cabbage, throw red pepper pods in cooking pan.

The White House Cook Book also had this rare recipe for Blueberry Pickles — Pick over berries and use only sound ones. Fill jars within one inch of top, then pour in enough molasses to settle down in all spaces — "this cannot be done in a moment, only lazy people will feel obliged to stand by and watch its progress." As it settles, pour in more until all berries are covered. Tie a piece of cloth over top and set in preserve closet (must not be kept air tight.) Wild grapes may be pickled in same manner.

About 1913, cookery of the Northwest came into its own when the Women of Portland published a cookbook which they said contained favorite recipes of the leading Northwest families. And sure enough, it held such wonders as Ben Holladay's Corn Bread: 1 pint of cornmeal, 1 tablespoon butter and 1 teaspoon salt, mix well after pouring boiling water over (doesn't say how much) to soften. Then break in yolks of 6 eggs, cool and add beaten whites of the eggs. Bake.

Another western wonder was described as "Sons of Rest Beefsteak" The instructions said to broil thick porterhouse steak rare, then score deeply with sharp knife. Spread with plenty of butter, sprinkle with salt and pepper. Pour sherry over, and spread top with mustard mixed with water. Put in oven for 15 minutes and serve.

Shrimp Wiggle was also popular in early days Oregon, according to the Portland Women's Cookbook. This was made by stirring 1 cup of cut-up shrimp into 1½ cups of rich cream sauce, along with a cup of green peas and 3 tablespoons of Madeira. Salt, pepper and mace were then added along with lemon juice. The mixture was heated and served. ●

Always an aritocrat, Pennoyer was never seen in public without his Henry Clay style standing collar. His manner was stiff and dignified, but he was always approachable by any voter.

Irishman Outwits Governor

Vying with Tom McCall for the title "Oregon's most colorful governor" is Sylvester Pennoyer, who like McCall served eight years as the state's Chief Executive.

Pennoyer took office in 1887 and served until 1895. Before that he was a Portland school teacher and the editor of a newspaper. He came out of retirement to run for governor, and for 10 years he was probably the most prominent man in Oregon — certainly the most conspicuous.

An outspoken man who often took unpopular stands which got him severely criticized, Pennoyer said he would "rather be abused than ignored" and some of his associates sometimes wondered if he didn't champion some cause just to create controversy.

Pennoyer was elected because of his position on the Chinese question at a time when labor was contending that the Chinese brought here to work on the railroads and in the gold mines had served their purpose and were taking their jobs. In his race for governor, Pennoyer defeated Colonel Thomas Cornelius, described as a worthy pioneer, but who had committed the "dire, unpardonable offense" of once hiring a Chinaman to wash some shirts. Pennoyer's people contended that this offense "showed a lack of sympathy for the laboring man."

After winning on the "masses against classes" platform, Pennoyer startled everyone by giving an inaugural address that attacked the Supreme Court and federal power in general. The states, he contended, should have supreme power to run their own affairs.

The object of his attack was a U.S. Supreme Court decision that had declared an alien registry law, aimed against the Chinese, as being unconstitutional.

This astonishing exposition of constitutional powers between the legislative and judicial branches of government was a fair example of what became known as "Pennoyerism." Those who knew the governor best said that his publicly-expressed opinions, especially those directed against the established order of things, were not always what he knew to be fact, but they never failed to touch some popular chord and win a following. And Pennoyer did want and did have a following

The Oregon Constitution forbids a man to occupy the position of chief executive for more than two consecutive terms of four years each, and in 1894 Pennoyer announced that he was going to run for U.S. Senator from Oregon. He was defeated, but during the campaign there was a funny incident.

Carrying his candidacy to the smallest towns in the state was characteristic of Pennoyer. One night he addressed the people at Heppner in Eastern Oregon. The next morning he took the train to the Junction, enroute to Arlington. He arrived at the Junction early, and discovered there was nothing there except the junction. It was nine miles to Arlington, and there were no trains running, nothing to do and no one to see.

Looking about, the Governor spotted a shack not far away which looked as if it might have an occupant. He walked up and rapped, but there was no response. Pounding harder, he finally succeeded in eliciting an inquiry made in a loud voice — "Who in the divil are you?''

The voice had a thick brogue that smacked of the Emerald Isle.

Pennoyer replied in his characteristically mild voice, ''I am Governor Pennoyer, and I would like to get a bite of breakfast.''

''Well,'' said the voice in the cabin, ''I've been up all night and I'm not going to get up now, not even fur a Guv'ner.''

When Pennoyer insisted that he let him in, at least, as there was no place to rest, the Irishman replied, ''Ah, go on wid ye! As ye said to President Cleveland, 'You attend to your business and I'll attend to mine.'''

This was too much for the Governor, and he had to laugh as he turned to Arlington and walked and carried his suitcase the entire nine miles, arriving completely exhausted.

It was true that Pennoyer had sent the same curt and undignified message repeated by the Irishman to the President of the United States a short time before, and it had been widely publicized. During the prevalence of the Coxey's Army Crusade, the president had advised the governors of the states as to their duties in the management of disorders, and on receiving this message, Governor Pennoyer replied:

To the President:

Yours is received. If you will attend to your business I will attend to mine.

Sylvester Pennoyer,
Governor of Oregon

Pennoyer's dislike of President Cleveland also prompted him to show his independence of the ''Great Apostate'' another time when he set a different day for the observance of Thanksgiving in Oregon than that named by the president. ●

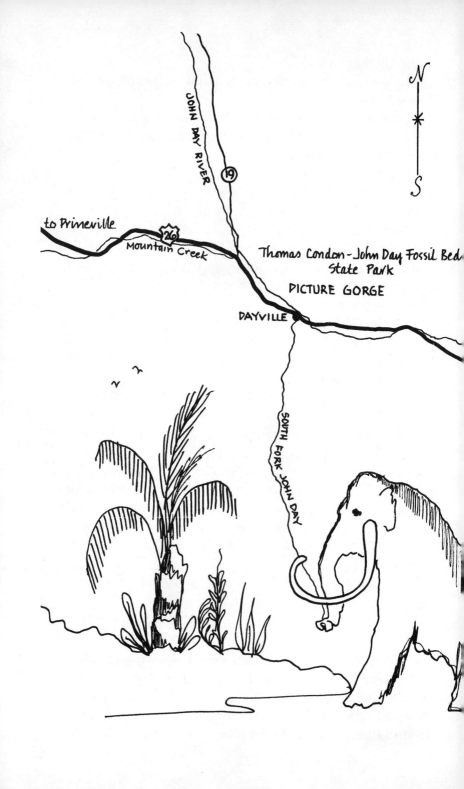

Oregon is 50 Million Years Old

Oregon has old stuff that can qualify as being some of the oldest things around. Some date back 50 million years!

During the last Century, the John Day fossil bed in Central Oregon attracted scientists from many parts of the country. Eastern colleges sent scientific expeditions here when there were still no roads, and the members of the parties worried about Indian raids.

Unfortunately, many of the fine fossil specimens from the John Day beds went into collections in other parts of the country, but some remain in private collections of local individuals. Only recently have some of the families with these collections begun to realize the importance of their specimens.

Scientists explain that the circumstances that led to the preservation of fossils in the extensive John Day area were a series of fortitious events enacted by Mother Nature.

First, John Day country was a semi-tropical land, damp and lush with teeming animal life, including animals that are extinct today. Among these were the tiny horses, possibly the ancient ancestors of some of today's equines, as well as a strange tree-climbing bear-dog, and many others.

Then, nature went into its mountain-building act, which resulted in the uplifting of the Cascade range. As the volcanoes exloded and poured out great flows of basalt and ash, the forests and the animals that had lived there were buried, and consequently preserved.

Thousands of years later, after things quieted down, rivers were formed and drainage basins, and the subsequent erosion led to the discovery of the ancient fossils, telltale evidence of events and life forms here in prehistoric times.

During the past year, the government has recognized the importance of preserving this evidence and has created the John Day National Fossil Monument.

With headquarters in the little town of John Day, the objective of the National Monument will be not only to protect the fossil beds from vandalism and unorganized digging, but it will also be to explain and interpret the wonders of the John Day fossils to the publc.

An interpretive center has been opened in a restored farmhouse a few miles out of John Day and overlooking some of the richest fossil beds in the world along the John Day river.

For persons who would still like to find some fossil specimens for their own collections, there remain a few places outside the state and federally-owned land where these can be dug. Most of these are on private land, and permission must be obtained from the owner.

However, most people agree that it is better to leave the undisturbed fossils where they are so that scientists will be able to do future studies that will perhaps tell us even more about our Northwest heritage. ●

"Slab-Sided Old Maid" Turns Tables

When Susan B. Anthony, famous woman suffragist, visited Portland in the summer of 1871 to advocate the vote for women, one of the city's well-known attorneys, Ben Halladay, helped pay her steamer fare here.

Large, friendly crowds attended her three lectures at the city's Oro Fino Theatre, and these audiences found her "soft-spoken, motherly and modestly attired," instead of the "cranky old maid" that she was caricatured to be in the papers of the day.

Following her speeches, the Portland daily papers published cold reports, despite the fact that she was well received there and in other cities she visited in the mid-Willamette Valley.

At the Oregon State Fair in Salem in September, Miss Anthony had some fun with one of her previous hecklers. Speaking in the open in the shade of the pavillion, she spotted a military man in the audience who had called her a "slab-sided old maid" in a newspaper article. The kidding he received before he escaped was reported to be exceedingly amusing to everyone but himself and he was not known therafter to repeat the offense.

From Salem, Miss Anthony traveled in style to Walla Walla as the invited guest of Captain J.C. Ainsworth on one of the OR & N palatial river steamers. Not all of her travels around Washington and Oregon were so luxurious, however, as she often was jostled on rough stagecoach roads or bounced from city to city in a buckboard.

The climax of her Northwest visit came when Miss Anthony and Abigail Scott Duniway, another suffragist, were invited to speak at the joint session of the Washington territorial legislature in Olympia. They were reported to be the first women officially invited to address that august body.

Mrs. Duniway, representing the Oregon State Woman Sufrage Association, carried on the peaceful battle for enfranchisement of women in both Oregon and Washington.

Twenty-five years after her first visit to Oregon, Miss Anthony returned to Portland "crowned with riches and fame." She was a particularly bright star at the first Oregon Congress of Women in 1896.

"The hour of woman's full and complete enfranchisement is not yet come." said the distinguished guest, "but it is coming. We have to but work and wait for it yet a little longer." ●

Molly Shoots 20 Indians

The pioneer Pritchard family picked out an isolated homestead on the Rogue River.

Their cabin sat at the head of a long, open meadow back among the trees.

One summer afternoon they noticed smoke coming from the direction of their nearest neighbors, and the Pritchards knew it was Indians.

They had two choices: make a run for the safety of

the town of Gold Beach, or stay and fight it out.

"This place is all we've got in the world. We're staying,' Pritchard told his wife.

They barricaded themselves in their cabin and the night passed into a new day.

With the first light, Molly Pritchard noticed shadows slinking from tree to tree. She whispered to her husband and then placed their child safely under the bed.

One hundred Indians swooped down on the cabin

and in the first charge, the white man inside was killed.

Without a moment for grieving, Molly scooped up the rifle and took her place beside the window.

She fired and an Indian fell. The braves retreated to the safety of the woods.

Again they ran across the clearing, whooping and howling in blood-curdling screams. Molly stood her ground and fired.

All day long, the Indians attacked and every charge they attempted was repulsed by the sure-shooting woman.

Sometimes she weakened and slumped to the floor, but each time she did the wild howls of the Indians and the cries of her child revived her and she resumed her post.

About four o'clock in the afternoon, Molly Pritchard heard a welcome sound — white men's voices and gunshots answering her own.

A party of settlers had come to her rescue, and around the cabin they found the bodies of 20 Indians the stout-hearted Molly Pritchard had killed. ●

"Hay-Burner" Unique Riverboat

The most unique craft ever to ply the waters of the Willamette River made its inaugural voyage in 1860.

Built by a man from Marysville and designed with economy in mind, it was an oxen-powered boat dubbed "The Hay Burner" by skeptics.

The two oxen "powered" the contraption by walking on a treadmill, and hay was the only "fuel" aboard.

On the boat's maiden voyage, it went aground at McGooglin's Slough after being launched near Independence. It remained aground until the oxen had eaten most of the fuel.

When it was finally pulled free and back into the current, The Hay Burner continued on downstream to its destination just above the Oregon City Falls without further mishap.

However, on the return trip, the current was too much for the oxen. The skipper abandoned his venture and sold the oxen.　●

Why Covered Bridges?

On Feb. 1, 1947, a severe windstorm hit the Willamette Valley, leaving wreck and havoc in its wake. The strong and steady winds beat away at trees and buildings, and Mother Nature won more than one battle with man's efforts that stormy night. Knight's Bridge, spanning the Molalla River near Canby, was lost to the storm. Already condemned to vehicular traffic and replaced with a modern span, its loss was not significant to commerce and travel, but was noted only because it was the oldest standing covered bridge in Oregon.

Built in 1877 by Albert Stuart Miller, Knight's Bridge was completed the same year a Lane County official complained that murder trials and the building of bridges were causing Lane County to more than double its expenses.

Knight's Bridge, one of many built by Miller using a specially patented truss designed by Robert W. Smith, took five months to complete at a total cost of $3,500.

Bridges in Oregon have progressed from the makeshift structures built by settlers for a single crossing, to private toll bridges sited at strategic crossing points, to those publicly financed after 1848 when a new law gave the counties authority to build bridges "at locations deemed suitable and appropriate."

Bridge building was about to come to its own as a big business.

The economics of bridge building were apparent to

everyone.

As early as 1861, H. McDonald advertised himself as an architect and bridge builder, and both Marion and Polk counties used his services.

It was Albert Stuart Miller of the firm A.S. Miller and Sons who distinguished himself as the dean of Oregon bridge builders. But bridge builders had to bid on specifications offered by the counties, and it was among county commissioners that the economics of a bridge building was often a heated issue.

Covered bridges were more expensive to build and to some folks, particularly those from other parts of the country where bridges had long life, the added expense was unnecessary.

But many county commissioners realized that open bridges tended to rot more quickly and that the extra expense of covering a bridge was more than made up for in the longer life of the span.

That lesson was not learned easily or rapidly. On June 5, 1909, a passenger train consisting of one engine and one coach was crossing the Currin Bridge on the Row River five miles east of Cottage Grove when the 90-foot truss supporting the bridge collapsed, causing the passenger coach to fall into the river about 25 feet below.

The Currin Bridge was an uncovered bridge built less than seven years before it collapsed. If it had been covered, it would have lasted 20 years, pointed out a Railroad Commission report.

All bridges on the railroad line were covered after that accident, but the incident dramatically illustrated the false economy of building uncovered bridges.

A few covered bridges were erected as recently as the late 1940s.

Several miles east of Cottage Grove across the Row River near the site of the collapse of the Currin Bridge in 1909, a new bridge was built in 1950. Two years later this bridge was covered, making it one of the most modern covered bridges in the United States.

In 1962 and 1963, two other covered bridges were built in Oregon, both for private use. They are the Rock-O-The-Range bridge across the Swalley Canal in Bend and the Milo Academy Bridge across the South Umpqua River in Milo.

It is not only their coverings or the arguments about whether they should be covered at all that distinguished Oregon bridges in the second half of the 19th Century.

Another distinctive feature of Oregon bridges is that they were built of native materials found at the bridge sites.

An account of the building of a covered bridge at Horse Creek about 55 miles up the McKenzie from Eugene indicates that a camp was set up and axes, adzes, shovels, picks, hand saws, splitting froes, sledges, splitting mauls, dollies, truss rods, augers, jacks, peavies, hammers, nails, ropes, hand winches, drift pins, rifles, shotguns and fishing equipment were brought to the camp.

No lumber was taken because all such material, including shingles and clapboards, were available from natural materials at the site.

About six to eight men were required for the job, and each man was expected to be able to do all parts of the work. Pay was $2.50 a day.

One of the crew members was cook. He had fresh fish and game and eggs and milk from nearby farms, and he turned the food into simple but hearty fare for the workers.

All the men helped with the dishes, then the cook joined the building crew until it was time to start the next meal.

No drinking or profanity were permitted in this

crew.

Undoubtedly Miller's greatest contribution to building in Oregon was not the use of the Smith truss, but the training of Lord Nelson Roney who built more than 100 covered bridges and in impressive list of commercial and religious buildings in the Willamette Valley.

Nels Roney got his first job as a bridge carpenter with Miller in 1876 and stayed with the firm until 1881, when a flood destroyed more covered bridges in Oregon than contractors could replace.

Roney formed his own company which continued to build well into the 20th Century.

The value and contribution of covered bridges to Oregon's economy and progress cannot be overstated, but well into this century the argument of to cover or not to cover still raged among bridge builders.

In 1916 the annual report of the state highway engineer included remarks that covered bridges were a fire hazard and a haven for tramps and holdups.

Also, the report claimed, many horses refused to cross covered bridges at night.

But 10 years later, samples were taken from a covered bridge built in 1874 and the timbers were found to be in an excellent state of preservation.

"The timbers, after 53 years of service, are undoubtedly stronger than they were when new. Douglas fir can be preserved in sound structural condition for at least half a century by the simple expedient of keeping it covered from the weather and providing for free circulation of air."

Durability and economy were not the only reasons bridges were covered, at least in some people's minds.

In 1862 an editorial appeared in the Salem Statesman noting the erection of the bridge at the south end of Salem across the South Mill Creek. ●

Bedticking Pants Save Justice

In early times the home of Robert Kinney in the Chehalem Valley was noted for having its doors open to all who passed. Among its guests were itinerant pioneer preachers, traveling salesmen, and even judges of the courts. These travelers were always welcome to warm at the huge fireplace, or take a

place at the family table.

On a day in the fall, when the Oregon rains were coming down with more than their usual deluge, a tall and stately man, picturesquely attired in sombrero hat and buckskin trousers with an elaborate side fringe, and with a long silken waist scarf of bright crimson topped with a heavy flannel shirt, came to the door.

The guest was His Honor Judge Pratt, Oregon's

first territorial judge — a man of fine personal appearance and impressive bearing. His Spanish-fashion attire, recently introduced from California, was saturated by the downpour and he was glad to seek shelter in the Kinney home.

After the judge had retired, Mrs. Kinney thoughtfully hung his rain-soaked pantaloons by the fire that they might dry before morning, which they did and more!

To those unacquainted with the peculiarities of wet buckskin should be explained that quick drying shrinks it unmercifully, and the judge's trousers shrank to such an extent that he could not possibly get into them. Having no others with him, the situation was grave, but Mrs. Kinney was equal to the emergency. Taking one of her blue and white striped bedticks, she quickly sewed a pair of trousers for the long-legged inactivated judge, and he reposed in bed until they were completed.

When they were ready, he gratefully put on the emergency trousers and left — perhaps not quite as picturesque as when he arrived, but able to proceed on his way to the next town to discharge the duties of his office. ●

N.W. Bedbugs Bite President

When they toured the Pacific Northwest in 1880, President Rutherford B. Hayes and General William T. Sherman made an overnight stop at the U.S. Hotel in Jacksonville, Oregon.

Preparations for the arrival of the president created a great deal of excitement in Jacksonville. His hotel room was kalsomined, a new rug was put down, and the room was even given a picture.

The visit went well, but when the bill for the one night stay was presented, Treasury Secretary John Sherman was aghast — it was over $100. He indignantly informed the proprietor that "the president merely desired a night's lodging and didn't want to buy the property."

Later, when he wrote his memoirs, President Hayes recalled that a large army of very active bedbugs had joined him in his suite in Jacksonville.

"Being a staunch Democrat, I didn't mind the excessive bill as much as 'sleeping with the entire Republican army,'" the president said. ●

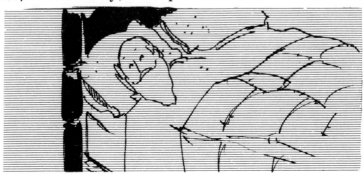

When Joe Meek went to Washington, D.C., to
carry Northwest Territory message about need for
help, he was without funds and dressed in rough
buckskins. Deciding to be 'just what he was,' he stayed in character and entranced Washington society
with wild and wooly tales of West. Few people who
saw him then would have recognized him in his pic-
ture-posing clothes as he is shown here.

Meek Hero of Champoeg

Joe Meek, famous mountain man of the Northwest, saved the day for law and order in the Oregon country at Champoeg in 1843, when he rallied residents of the Willamette Valley and talked them into organizing the first government in the frontier wilderness of Oregon.

Champoeg, the site of this historical meeting is today an Oregon State Park with an impressive newly-opened Visitors Center that details the history of the area.

The historic 1843 meeting was held because of growing concern about who should govern this part of the Northwest. The arrival of the first white men in the early 1800s had resulted in a treaty of joint occupation, signed in 1818, to allow settlement of the region.

The British and French-Canadians felt they had a prior right to the Oregon Country because of their extensive exploration throughout the region as part of the fur trade, and the establishment of the large and powerful Hudson's Bay Company post at Fort Vancouver on the Columbia River. American claims were based on Captain Robert Gray's discovery of the Columbia River in 1792, and the presence of the Lewis and Clark Expedition along the Columbia in 1805-1805.

As the number of American settlers continued to grow, they became increasingly concerned about the establishment of some form of civil government. Beginning in 1841, a series of meetings of settlers began to devise a proposal for the establishment of an American government, and at the now famous gathering of settlers, both American and French-Canadian, at Champoeg on May 2, 1843, the proposal was ready.

A hundred or so people were present, about half the adult male population of the Willamette Valley. The report from the earlier meetings of American settlers called for the people "to organize themselves into a civil community, and provide themselves with the protection" of law and order. At first the proposal was rejected, with most of the French-Canadians voting against it. Then came a suggestion to divide the voters into two groups so that an actual count of the close vote could be made. It was at this point that Joe Meek steped forward and shouted, "Who's for a divide? All for the organization, follow me."

When heads were counted, the tally was 52 votes for organization, 50 against. Meek's reputation and the force of his personality doubtless was an important, perhaps a crucial, influence.

Officers of the fledgling government were then elected, and a committee chosen to draft a code of laws. These were adopted at Champoeg a couple of months later and became Oregon's first written constitution.

The importance of Champoeg as a political center ended in 1844 when the Provisional Government was established at Oregon City. But for the next 15 years, Champoeg was an important commercial and transportation center because of its strategic location above the falls on the Willamette River. The town was the port of call for steamboats and other river craft carrying passengers and freight to and from the farms and towns in the mid-Willamette Valley. It was also a regular stop on the several valley stage lines.

Champoeg was platted as a townsite in 1852, and

became a bustling village of about 30 buildings, including a schoolhouse, Masonic Hall, bowling alley, livery stable, warehouses, saloons, hotel and a church. It enjoyed a reputation as a rough and rugged town and business in the saloons thrived.

Before the white men came, Champoeg had also been a trade and population center for Indians of the Kalapooian tribe. It was the only place where there was an opening in the thick forests which grew along the river, and was a popular village where the Indians came to hunt, fish, trade, pick berries and socialize.

As the frontier town grew, many of the Indians remained, and Indians gambling in the streets or engaging in an occasional drunken brawl enlivened routine life of the town. By 1860, the estimated population of Champoeg was about 180 persons, with many others living on farms in the nearby area.

Then came the disastrous flood of 1861. It completely destroyed the town. Heavy rains and melting snow during November pushed the river over its banks until it stood 30 feet deep in parts of the town. The current was so swift that no buildings, except the sturdy old Hudson Bay trading post, survived — and it was moved fifty yards off its foundations.

Champoeg was never rebuilt, although during the next 20 years several warehouses, a dock, a flour mill and a sawmill operated there. The town remained an important shipping point for produce from Willamette Valley farms.

Another flood in 1890, almost as bad as the 1861 flood, swept away those buildings too, and in 1892, the townsite was officially abandoned.

The historical significance of Champoeg was first recognized in 1901, when a square rod of land was donated to the state for a Memorial Park. A monument commemorating the Oregon pioneers who voted to establish the provisional government was dedicated the same year. Since then, there have been many arguments and a continuing controversy among historians and historical groups about exact geography of the site.

But in 1943, Champoeg was designated a State Park, and with completion of the new visitors' center it has been officially recognized as the "Birthplace of Oregon Government."

In addition to being a historic site, the park also provides two picnic areas and an overnight camp — a combination which makes it unique in the Oregon State Park system. ●

Recently Champoeg, on the Willamette River near Wilsonville, has been recognized as the "birthplace of Oregon government." Displays at the Champoeg State Park provide details for history buffs.

19-Year-Old Commander Was Winner

A 19-year-old was the commander of one of the American ships to make the hazardous voyage around the tip of Africa and to the Northwest and the Orient in 1794-95.

John Boit was the young commander's name and his ship was the "Union." It was a 98-ton sloop, about 50 or 60 feet long.

Sailing out of Newport, Rhode Island, on August 11, 1794, the Union arrived in Puget Sound on May 16, 1795, a passage of 260 days.

On the West Coast, young Boit traded successfully with the Indians during the summer and on September 12, 1795, departed for Boston by way of the Sandwich (Hawaiian) Islands and China. He reached Boston with a cargo of furs and Oriental goods on July 8, 1796.

"Arrived sloop Union-Boit-Canton," was the only notice taken by Boston papers of this remarkable exploit of a boy of 19 years.

ADDIS CRANDALL GIBBS

Gov. Gibbs Saves Oregon for Union

If it hadn't been for the alertness of its Civil War governor, Addis Crandall Gibbs, Oregon might have been one of the states taken over by the Confederacy.

A conspiracy of Friends of the Confederacy made plans to take the undefended state of Oregon out of the Union, but Governor Gibbs found out about the plot and was able to thwart it.

His vigilance was afterwards described by one of the plotters: "Yes, Gibbs got the best of us, and as things have turned out, I'm glad of it."

Gibbs came to the North Umpqua valley from California in 1851 and took up a donation claim at what is now Gardiner. He obtained a U.S. mail contract, bought a cayuse pony, and with a flour sack for a mail pouch, carried the first U.S. mail across the Calapooya Mountains into the valley of the Umpqua.

On these trips, the mail carrier was hailed as he passed the isolated cabins, stopped. Taking his flour sack mailbag into the cabin, he emptied it and let each person select his own mail. Then he tied up what was left and proceeded to the next cabin.

A short time after initiating the mail route, however, Gibbs sublet it, and accepted an appointment as Collector of Customs for the District of Cape Perpetua, which included Coos Bay and the Umpqua River, with the office located at Gardiner.

In 1858, Gibbs came to Portland with his bride of four years, and started to practice his old profession of the law. He was an active member of theTaylor Street Methodist Church and was for many years president of its board of trustees. For a long time he headed the board of trustees of Willamette University at Salem. He represented Umpqua County in the Territorial legislature and became a member of the state legislature in 1860. In 1862, he was elected governor of the state.

After the war, Governor Gibbs turned his attention to locating state school lands and is credited with the reservation of ten thousand acres. This was the first move in the state toward a perpetual school fund.

Following his failure to be chosen U.S. Senator, Gibbs served several terms as district prosecuting attorney and as U.S. Attorney. He moved to England in 1884, where he died in 1886.

The Oregon legislature had his body returned to the state, and he is buried in Riverview Cemetery in Portland. ●

Lost Village of Coast Range

It is rumored that somewhere on the flat top of a steep promontory in the Oregon Coast Range is the remains of an Indian village which dates back hundreds of years before the discovery of the West Coast of Oregon and Washington by white men.

One of the early surveyors for a railroad route across Oregon heard a story about the prehistoric settlement from members of tribes who lived in the Willamette Valley at the time of the survey.

In those days the Indians recounted legends about the village, but refused to go near its reported site. It was ancient, the surveyor was told, dating back far beyond the memories of the oldest members of the tribe and beyond the memories of their fathers, or their grandfathers.

Location of the legendary village was ideal, the Indians said. It was inaccessible except by one rout,e because of the steepness and ruggedness of the terrain. It had a source of fresh water and was almost impregnable against attack.

Writing later in a book about his survey, the author describes how he believes he found the site after several days of searching for a route to reach a mountainous promontory.

The place answered the description the Indians had given him, and there was indication that the earth had been excavated much earlier and had a system of connecting trenches which he thought may have linked the various habitations together. From the condition of the area when he visited in the early 1800s, the surveyor concluded that the village, if this was the site, must indeed be ancient.

With recently discovered evidence that the West Coast has been inhabited by humans for at least 10,000 years, interest in these earlier cultures is increasing. Who knows what treasures will be found or what artifacts will be located that will give us a better understanding of the people who enjoyed the Oregon country in earlier days? ●

Pioneers Had Their UFO

An old book written about early history in the Northwest reveals a strange story written by an E.L. Kimmel, who came here in 1902.

In view of strange tales about UFO's (unidentified flying objects) and other unexplained phenomena, Mr. Kimmel's tale seems to fit right in. He tells of a strange light that was seen by many in the vicinity of the family homestead in the Rattlesnake Hills southeast of Yakima, Wash.

"It was a light that could be seen, but never explained," Kimmel says.

So frequent was its appearance, that it was dubbed the "Golden Horseman" by many residents of the

vicinity.

"Sometimes it looked like two lights and would jump across the canyon, and at times it would move along like a dog hunting mice," he recalls.

The light was always seen in the same vicinity, within about a mile of a popular waterhole.

One time when Kimmel was riding along the area about dusk, he said the light jumped out from behind a sagebrush not more than 20 feet away from him and leaped to a hillside about a quarter mile distant and then moved as if hunting.

Other strange things happened in the same vicinity. One morning a huge rock that was half buried along the pony trail was found rolled out of place and turned upside down. Animals in the area often became frightened for no apparent reason, Kimmel says.

Another time, he and his father dug a well 16 feet deep and cribbed it with two-by-sixes. Six months later the cribbing was found one morning laying "all twisted in the bottom of the well, most of it broken in the center, but the sides of the well which consisted of stone and earth were not disturbed."

So it seems that every generation has its strange phenomena — weird, irrational sights and events that are never understood or explained. ●

Wild Steers Made Cowboys Tough

Oregon and eastern Washington had its share of cowboys. Just like in Western novels, they rode the ranges, stalked the dusty streets of cowtowns, and fought with the sheepherders.

But the real cowboy of this country actually only existed for about 40 or 50 years, although you may still find a few who qualify for the title on the big ranches east of the Cascade mountains. Their real hey-day, however, was from the end of the Civil War to about the beginning of the 20th Century.

Western cowboys got tough and earned their reputations mostly because of the Longhorn and the

wild Mexican cattle that were driven into this country shortly after the first settlers got their cabins built.

Longhorns and the Mexican cattle were the roughest, toughest "critters" that man ever tried to domesticate enough to market. They had the ability to stay alive on lands where other cattle would starve to death. Descended from tough Andalusian cattle brought to the New World in the early 16th Century from Spain, they were hard cattle to round up and drive, or to brand.

Because their meat was not very good quality, they were mostly valued for their hides, horns, hooves and tallow, so young "cowboys," who might work for as little as $5 a month were often used to drive the cattle. As the cattle industry grew up, the age of the cowboys seemed to increase, but it still remained, essentially a young man's game.

Cowboys had immense loyalty to the outfit they worked for, and often voiced owners contempt for the sheepmen who drove large bands of sheep to and from the valley and mountains to graze. In Eastern Oregon, there were many bitter incidents, and clashes between the two.

The cowboy usually had his own saddle, bridle and bedroll, and a few had their own horse, but usually the employer furnished the horses and everything else. Bunkhouses were the places where the cowboys lived when they were working out of a central ranch and, like loggers, they ate in a central cookhouse, usually with a Chinese cook in the early days of the Northwest.

When the outfit was on the move, rounding up, or driving cattle, the cowboys slept under the stars and ate out of a chuckwagon, which rolled along with the drive.

In Southeast Oregon, as in other places, the cowboy washed his clothes and took a bath only when it was convenient. Sometimes, it wasn't until he "went into town." Othertimes, he found bathing places provided by nature. One such place was in the middle of the Alvord Desert in the shadow of Steens Mountain. It was a hotspring.

For years, this particular spring had alongside it one of the old handle-operated washing machines. The cowboy who rode by could fill the tub with water, dump his clothes in and work the handle until they were clean enough to suit him. Then he could hang them to dry on the sagebrush and jump in the hotsprings for a bath.

Someone had thoughtfully carved a bathtub out of the clay at the springs. When his clothes were dry, he could jump back on his horse and be on his way.

The wild Mexican cattle and the Longhorns disappeared from the cattle markets as homesteaders fenced in the open range and more domesticated brands of beef cattle began arriving in the Northwest. These cattle were not the stuff legends were made of, and gradually the cowboy, too, began to disappear except in those parts of the country where there was still lots of open range and BLM lands. Even in these area, his image changed, although the legends of the Old West still live on.

The cowboy is the center of those legends. He remains tough, courageous, and colorful and we think of him fondly, much like the English think of their knights of old. ●

Maryhill Museum, rising impressively among barren hills above Columbia River Gorge, was originally intended to be a family mansion. When that dream faded, Sam Hill had another dream — one that materialized.

Sam's Dream House

Maryhill Museum, high on a hill overlooking the Columbia River near Goldendale in Eastern Washington, is said to be the results of a man's dream.

Now, some dreams are nightmares, and some turn out to be interesting and unusual even though they are a little bizarre. Maryhill is the pleasant type of dream, still mysterious and puzzling, but filled with unique and exciting things — like an old trunk in the attic!

However, in 1914, when Sam Hill, the railroad magnate, began building a huge concrete "chateau" on the lonely, isolated and windswept banks of the Columbia, the nearby residents of Goldendale called the project "nightmarish."

Had Sam Hill gone mad? Or was he building a private asylum for a mad relative? Why were the walls so massive? Why such a grand structure in such an isolated place?

Hill had brighter visions. He thought the region was a perfect climate — just the right balance between aridity and humidity. He thought the area was going to grow, and it seemed the perfect place to live.

However, before the building was finished, Hill changed his mind. A friend, Loie Fuller, the "little artist woman," talked him into finishing the structure as a museum of art. A tribute to artistry and a place to house fine collections.

Loie had caught Hill's attention because at the time she was the living embodiment of the "Art

Nouveau'' movement that was sweeping the country.

From humble beginnings (she was born in a bar in Illinois because this was the only warm place for her mother to give birth in the freezing Illinois winter), Loie had, by her own efforts, risen to great heights of popularity as a dancer.

Discovering that remarkable visual effects could be created with long flowing robes and lighting, the rather dumpy Loie had produced a new form of dance that caught on. Rebuffed by a refusal at the Paris Opera, she went to the Folies Bergere and captured audiences there with her swirling draperies.

When Hill announced that his eastern Washington structure was to be a museum, the people in the wilds of the country were sure he had really lost his mind. Building an expensive mansion in the middle of nowhere was odd enough, but a museum was even odder.

Twelve years passed. The museum was completed and many friends of Loie and Hill donated works of art, or money for collections to add to those supplied by the two, but there they sat.

Then one day word came that Marie, the Queen of Romania was coming to Maryhill to dedicate the museum!

Everyone was excited. Why was such an important personage coming to the wild and remote place to dedicate a museum? Gossip flourished, as almost everyone in both Washington and Oregon speculated.

No one knows for sure why Marie came, but she did, and the official story was that both Hill and Loie had helped Romania during the suffering there in the First World War, and Marie was grateful. In her dedication speech, Queen Marie answered some of the unkind remarks about her peculiar destination.

"Sam Hill is building not only for today, but for

tomorrow," she said. "There is much more in this building made of concrete than we can see. There is a dream built into this place.

"Some may smile and scoff, for they do not understand, but I came in understanding of his dream."

As the years go by, the collections at Maryhill get more valuable, and it becomes more interesting to visit the museum. There are pieces by the sculptor Rodin, art glass by Emile Galle, and one of the best collections of Indian basketry in the world.

Then there is the collection given by Queen Marie — fine gold-leaf furniture from the palaces, and the gown and train worn by her at the coronations of Edward VII and Czar Nicholas II.

Maryhill is an interesting dream come true — a place for people to take a look at the past and enjoy it.

The Wolf Creek Tavern, a delightful bit of Oregon's past, has been saved and restored by the State Parks and Recreation Division.

Located just off Interstate 5, 20 miles north of Grants Pass at Wolf Creek, the historic tavern operates today as a restaurant and hotel, and is well worth a visit.

Glad To See That Tavern

Built in 1857, or thereabouts, the Wolf Creek Tavern has a colorful past, with many romantic stories told about it. One persistent legend says it was built by Ben Holladay, the Portland railroad and stagecoach baron, who also is said to have built several other stagecoach stations on the old Portland-Sacramento route. Others say that Chinese laborers built the Tavern over the tailings of an old gold mine. Still a third story contends that the original Wolf Creek Tavern burned in 1861 and was reconstructed immediately on the same foundation.

Operating By Mid-'70s

Some historical records indicate the Tavern was built between 1868 and 1873 by a local entrepreneur, Henry Smith, and was operating by the mid-1870s as a stopover for stages enroute to Portland and Sacramento.

In any case, the Tavern surely housed many a weary stagecoach passenger who made the 710-mile wagon road trip that took six days to cover the distance from city to city.

Stages left Portland and Sacramento at 6 a.m. every day carrying mail, passengers and baggage. In order to maintain the service, 28 coaches, 30 stage wagons and 500 horses were required.

Unique among other surviving Oregon stage coach stations, the Wolf Creek Tavern has remained in almost continuous operation over the years for essentially its original purpose.

A number of celebrities reportedly have stayed at

the Wolf Creek Tavern, among them U.S. President Rutherford B. Hayes who was traveling through Oregon in the 1880s. Other guests included Jack London and his wife, Charmain. London finished typing the "End of the Story" while staying there. Author Sinclair Lewis and movie star Mary Pickford and Clark Gable were among were recent guests.

State Acquires Tavern

The state acquired the Tavern in 1976, and did careful research to enable its restoration in order to portray its evolutionary changes and adaptations as a roadside inn. It is furnished with appropriate antiques and authentic reproductions.

Care has even been taken to reproduce original paint colors on walls, woodwork and chimneys. Whenever possible, the original woods and other original finishes have been left. The north room still bears boot marks on the fireplace where men propped up their feet to warm them near the fire.

Today, the Wolf Creek Tavern's innkeepers are Vernon and Donna Wiard who lease it from the Parks and Recreation Division. They are preserving the historic integrity of the building's original function and provide a warm and friendly welcome to guests, as has been the custom for more than 100 years. ⌐ ●

Moral — Keep End in View

When the first locomotive in Portland puffed down Fourth Street for the first time, a big Newfoundland dog rushed out with furious bark, snap and growl, as if to stop and scare the noisy critter away.

In darting back and forth in front of the snorting monster, he forgot to keep his tail out of the way and the engine inadvertently tramped on it, making him a bob-tailed dog in a wink of the eye. Otherwise, the dog was unhurt, and the incident inspired an unknown Oregon poet of the time to pen the following which appeared in the Oregon Journal a few days later, titled simply —

AN OREGON POEM

Attention, friends and hear my tale
About a dog who lost his tail:
And though this news shall be retailed.
That dog will never be re-tailed.
In Portland town the scene is laid.
Where late the Irish Pick brigade
Has built a railroad through the town
On which the cars go thundering down.
'Twas something new beneath the sun
To see the iron horse thus run
With snort and neigh and flying feet,
Adown the city's public street.
Our canine friend the breed mistook:
He had not read a breeder's book:
He thought it was a scrub cayuse
That thus was running wildly loose.

Now, being of that turn of mind
To do whate'er he felt inclined,
To aid the man who keeps the Pound,
He thought he'd chase the cayuse around:
So, with a fiercely savage roar,
He bounded on the track before
That snorting horse — that plunging steed —
And tried his best to check its speed.
Unmindful of his latter end,
(Something like you and me, my friend).
He ran about and fiercely bayed,
As though he meant to be obeyed.
But all at once he felt quite queer;
A wondrous lightness in the rear:
On looking round he soon did find
His narrative he'd left behind.
He'd crossed the track just once too oft:
That fiery steed, with head aloft,
Had nipped his tail off near his rump
And left him but a bloody stump.
No more can he, in doggish pride,
With Madame Canine by his side,
Parade the streets, his plume on high,
To catch the breezes wafting by.
That silky plume, now smeared with gore,
Can wave above his back no more:
It graces now the bloody field
Where he, at length, was forced to yield.
His colors fly at half-mast now,
And on his honest, canine brow,
We read this warning, meant for you,
'Tis, "keep your latter end in view."

75 Fishwheels Caught Salmon

At one time in the early 1900s, more than 75 fishwheels operated on the Columbia River. These were the days when heavy runs of salmon swam upstream to spawn — the days before the dams.

The ingenious fishwheels were an easy way to scoop the salmon out of the river, so they could be sent along to the processing plant. The fishwheels measured up to 45 feet in diameter, and were turned

by the force of the river's current. The fish were scooped out of the water in rotating dip net buckets.

One of the earliest operators of a fishwheel was Joseph (French) Latourell, who came around the Horn in a whaler. In 1859, he married Grace Ough, a grandaughter of an Indian chief, and settled at the site now officially named Latourell Falls on the

Columbia near where Rooster Rock State Park is now located.

Latourell, whose marriage was performed by Factor McLoughlin of the Hudson Bay Post, was credited with helping, because of his marriage, to create peace between the whites and the Indians. He was later a barge pilot, and he played fiddle at local dances.

About 10 miles further upstream, at Warrendale, the most prominent mid-Columbia River fish cannery was established in 1870. It processed the tons of fish caught by the fishwheels in this part of the river. The owner and pioneer packer was Frank M. Warren, who later was a victim of the Titanic disaster. The cannery processed up to 50,000 cases annually of salmon gathered by the entrapments.

Oregon outlawed fishwhels in 1926, and Washington followed suit in 1934. The wheels have disppeared, and few traces of this once large industry remain.

There is a historic marker near the entrance to Latourell Falls Trail and a cannery site marker on a utility pole Number 23 on the right side of the road at Warrendale, just across the river from Beacon Rock.

●

Where Was Pocahontas Oregon?

Not many persons know about it, but Oregon once had a town named in honor of Pocahontas, the Indian woman whose name became famous in connection with an early tale about the Pilgrims. The town of Pocahontas was near gold strikes on the Salmon and Marble Creeks in Eastern Oregon. At one time it was in the running to be the state capital of Oregon!

In those days, 1864, it was an important little town

Pocahontas. *Harper's*

with a hotel, express office, blacksmith shop and schoolhouse. When Pocahontas was nominated as a site for the state capital, it didn't receive many votes, but the publicity it received helped put it on the map for a time. In the voting, Salem won the selection with 6,108 votes, Portland received 3,854 votes, and Pocahontas got 10 votes.

After the gold rush subsided, Pocahontas dwindled

and finally vanished from the map. The schoolhouse was the last to go, even though it was on the main road to Haines and North Powder. Today, "Pocahontas Road" is about all that remains to mark the memory of the little town.

As for its namesake, Pocahontas herself, she was converted to Christianity by English colonists after her Indian husband died and she returned to the East. She married a John Rolfe who took her to England where she was welcomed as an Indian Princess and as royalty, and was received at the Court of St. James's.

However, she became homesick and wanted to come home, and when she was at last able to make that voyage, she was taken ill shortly after the ship embarked and died before it reached the sea. She was buried at St. George's Church at Graveshead. Later a little park with her statue and a sign was erected and the park was named Princess Pocahontas Gardens in her honor. ●

Big Raid Yields Bootleg Whiskey

Police came down on the criminals like a shoe on an ant. The round-up was in Portland February 20, 1923.

At the soft drink stand of Fred Baerer, 224 First Street, the barkeep was arrested for selling fortified grape juice. The tip-off was an advertisement about

wild grape juice in the front window, "a little bit will do you."

Across the river in east Portland, police walked in the Princess Hotel. The raid went so quickly that guests suddenly found plain-clothes officers standing beside them. Two women mistook the police for heistmen and came on with fingernails bared. Subdued and arrested the women gave away 16 pints of moonshine.

The north end of town produced a warehouse

where 458 pints were found. Although it was suspected that the two arrested were only two-bit characters no one bigger was brought in. Pete Killivich and Mike Vidish went up on charges of transporting and possessing liquor.

One of the smaller fish caught in the police dragnet was Joe Gramm. He bumped into officers at Fifth and Burnside and because of guilty actions his suitcase was searched. Inside were three gallons of whiskey wrapped in newspaper.

Of all the arrests that evening none is quite as sad as that of Mike Skulzi, a fifteen-year-old boy. He told his story: "You don't have to run a still every day in order to know how to make moonshine. We make it every two or three days, ten gallons at a time. I think I am still a good American."

According to the law the boy was far from good citizenship but the reasons for committing the offense: "My father walked out on us and hasn't given mother a cent in five years. Three months ago she went to work as a housekeeper. They never paid her.

"What else was there to do?"

Mike Skulzi, the boy immigrant from Dalmatia, was sent back to school where he left off — sixth grade.

The last bust Portland police made on that night of thirteen arrests was for dope, not booze. Jung Tung, a Chinese immigrant, was arrested for selling opium to an undercover policeman. ●

How Walnuts Came to N.W.

Walnuts are an important crop in Oregon, and the first ones ever planted here were brought from Indiana's Wabash Valley to this area about 125 years

ago.

Samuel K. Barlow, who built Oregon's first wagon road — the Barlow Road, across the Cascades — is the man responsible for transplanting walnuts to Oregon.

He came here from Indiana in 1845 and settled on a beautiful small prairie just south of Oregon City, which is still known as Barlow's Prairie. After a few years in his new home, he began to yearn for the big spreading walnut trees that had been abundant in his home state.

Determined to see if walnuts, which are not indigenous to Oregon, would grow here, he asked Oregon's first delegate to Congress, Samuel R. Thurston — who was elected in 1849 — to bring back a bag of walnuts with him when he returned to Oregon from Washington, D.C.

Barlow arranged to have a bushel of walnuts delivered to Thurston in Washington by his people in Indiana. Thurston served his term and started back to Oregon, but he died at sea on the return voyage, between Panama and Acapulco.

Barlow did not hear of his walnuts or their fate until several months later, and he presumed them lost. Then he received word from an agent in Portland that a bag of something with his name on it was being held in storage at the express office. Oh, and there was a $50 charge against if for freight.

Barlow replied that he would not pay such an outrageous price for a bag of walnuts and told the agent to keep them for the debt.

But about a week later, he relented, went to Portland, paid the freight bill — and took his walnuts home.

That fall, he planted them, and almost all of them grew. Within two years, he had sold over a hundred walnut trees at a dollar each. He had enough left to line a long drive from his house to the road. Not only did that pay his freight bill, but he doubled his money, started the walnut business in Oregon, and got all the beloved walnut trees he wanted for his own.

Years later, many of the original Barlow walnut trees still stood as venerable giants of their kind, and thousands of Oregon's other walnut trees can trace their ancestry back to the Barlow importation. ●

SPEAKING OF TREES!

This one with 12 men and a dog standing on its stump was an Oregon native. Many early residents who came west from the plains and wanted to farm wondered how to get rid of the monster trees.

Oregon Trunk Railway up Deschutes River canyon wasn't completed until 1911 when James G. Hill drove golden spike.

Getting Roads Was Rough

The first wagon road constructed to let people into the great Oregon territory has been used continuously since its original location in 1845. It is the route over the Cascade Range south of Mt. Hood known as the "Barlow Road."

It was located by Joel Palmer and Samuel K. Barlow, and much of the distance over the mountains was initiated in great danger and distress by starving, freezing immigrants in 1845. The old Barlow Road was also one of the first roads to receive a charter from the provisional government, and the only one constructed under such a charter.

The road leading from the east into southern Oregon was opened subsequent to the Barlow route, and was mainly the work of the Applegates, who settled in the Umpqua Valley. The greater portion of it, like the "Oregon Trail," was in no sense a constructed road, but a dim, general route passing over open ground.

With the organization of the Territorial Legislature, interest in constructing additional free highways was expressed, along with the desire for free schools.

The notion of developing a railroad in Oregon did not emerge until the early 1860s. By then there were about 60,000 persons in Oregon. The first tangible effort, continuously pushed until the actual construction of a railroad was commenced, started at Jacksonville, in southern Oregon, in 1864.

The year before, two surveyors, S.G. Elliot and

George H. Beldon, contributed their efforts to make a preliminary survey for a railroad from Marysvile, California, to Portland. These two men organized a survey party and without means or money made the survey, locating just about the same route as that used when the Oregon and California line was finally constructed.

However, the pair quarreled and abandoned the enterprise, leaving their men with five months' unpaid wages. Col. A.C. Barry, when Belden and Elliot deserted, put the whole party into the Jacksonville Hospital for the winter and then made the rounds of the town to arouse interest in raising money to continue the survey.

When he received some assurances of support, Barry proceeded to the Willamette Valley, going all the way from Jacksonville to Portland on foot, to enlist others in the project to complete the survey.

Without the help of J. Gaston, a Jacksonville attorney — who advanced money to pay members of the survey party under a contract pledging that they would continue work the next season — it is doubtful the survey would have been completed in late October of 1864. Gaston was also busy circulating and memorials, and urging Oregon Congressmen to get federal lands granted to support construction of the Oregon and California Railroad.

On July 25, 1866, Congress passed the act granting the lands. A second grant was made in 1870.

With proceeds from the first grant, the railroad was built from Portland to the southern boundary of the state, and the second grant provided the means to build the track from Portland to McMinnville. ●

House on Mt. Hood's Tip-Top

Not too many people remember that there once was a house right smack-dab on the summit of Mt. Hood.

It was built in 1915 by the U.S. Forest Service at a cost of $632.92 plus a lot of hard, back-breaking packing and carrying by Lige Coalman, the Iron Man of Hood, and others.

Coalman, who was very much at home on Mt. Hood's slopes or its summit, instigated the construction as a site for one of the new "Firefinder" devices, a map with a pivot point at the position of the given lookout station. The firefinder allowed rangers to take a bearing, and determine the exact location of

forest fires in the area.

Lumber for the summit house was pre-cut, and the four tons of boards and hardware were packed to the top of the mountain in 8 days with the help of a number of "packrats" paid about $5 a day. Before the hazardous packing over black ice and across several crevasses was complete, most of the men had quit, and it is reported that Coalman carried 120 pounds of nails and hardware up on the last load.

After its completion, the summit house was manned for 19 seasons, or until 1933, with the summit rangers usually giving hot coffee and hospitality to cold, weary climbers.

Coalman was the summit man for four years and during this time he participated in a number of spectacular rescues. By combining glissades, kangaroo leaps and much daring, he was clocked several times as coming down the mountain from the summit to Crater Rock in 6 minutes, a trip that usually took at least an hour.

In 1932, the Oregonian carried a news story saying that Mack Hall, the current summit ranger was hungry for eggs and would pay 35 cents a dozen for any brought to him. Response was prompt, guides and climbers alike began bringing eggs. Before the week was out, Hall was wondering what to do with 13 dozen eggs.

The house on Mt. Hood's summit was last manned in 1933, but plans were made for a new cabin on the summit and in 1940 materials were sent up the mountain to rebuild the summit cabin. However, it never was completed and a sudden storm in September that year brought an end to construction, and later the whole concept was abandoned.   ●

Barb Wire Tamed West

The Northwest has millions, perhaps billions of acres of barbed wire, but when the covered wagons first came to Oregon and the Northwest territory, there was no barbed wire.

Early settlers in the Willamette Valley, Cowlitz Prairie, and the early wheat ranchers east of the Cascade mountains had to figure out other ways of protecting their homesteads. These settlers came with the covered wagon migration which reached its peak around 1843-45, and continued for the next 30 years. It wasn't until after 1873 that barbed wire was invented and became available.

Collectors of barbed wire today see it as a symbol of the history and romance of the Old West. They can hear the shots fired by cowmen guarding their lands from sheepmen, and they claim that the West was really tamed by barbed wire.

And it is true that barbed wire was used by squatters and homesteaders alike to protect land and valuable water sources from marauding cattle. It was resented by cattlemen with free-ranging cattle. The result — it started many a range war.

Invented in France earlier, it was not until about 1873 that an American, Henry Rose, patented a kind of wire fencing that became popular.

A recent book on the subject states that more than 4,000 types of barbed wire are known. The rarest and most sought-after types carry such colorful names as "Hanging Knot," "Kelly's Thorny Fence," "Meriwether's Snake," "Stover Clip" and "Concertina

Steel.''

It is estimated there are more than 150,000 barbed wire collectors in the United States. In addition, there are dealers who deal principally in barbed wire, collectors' clubs and several publications devoted to the subject.

Wire is collected in 18-inch lengths, and often collections are displayed in attractive cases. Texas is the country's wire collectors' center, and the Texas Barbed Wire Collectors Association publishes a journal called "The Barbarian." ●

Horrifying Old Punishments

Take a look at the means of punishment and penalties dealt out by our self-righteous ancestors, and be glad that you live in this day and age.

Nathaniel Hawthorne, in "The Scarlet Letter," disclosed the mortification Hester Prynne suffered for her indiscretions — it was a scarlet "A"

emblazoned on her bosom for all to see. But this was probably among the least painful of the many penalties imposed.

All sorts of horrifying early punishments were given offenders of the community, the church, the military and the neighbors. Present-day penal codes may need improving, but the worst can't hold a candle to those of the past century.

The offenses dealt with through these extraordinary measures were as varied and weird as the punishments meted out. Nagging, swearing, drunkenness, stealing a pig, lying, wife-beating, fortune-telling and even ballad singing were among the indiscretions punishable by gruesome means.

In some towns, the pillory still remains on the village green as an item of historic interest. Seldom do the plaques mention that the offender's ears were nailed to the pillory during his stay and that they were slit free on release.

England, in particular, devised some nasty ways of punishing people, and the early settlers in America brought many of these along with them. Besides, our forefathers thought up some dandies of their own.

The bilboes, ducking stool, stocks, pillory, whipping post, scarlet letter, and public penance were among the milder punishments. Branding and maiming and tortures were frequently carried out by the military.

In Salem, they burned persons suspected of being witches. West Coast pioneers, angry at Chinese laborers, who they said were taking away their jobs, lassooed many from horseback and dragged them down the streets. Indians — men, women and children — were frequently shot on sight, and at least one incident chronicled in Oregon history tells how a respected captain of our military came upon a group of defenseless Indian women and children picking berries and ordered them all shot.

Among themselves, Indians of different tribes often behaved even worse. They took slaves when they raided neighboring villages, and frequently taunted and tortured their captives. ●

Costly Kettle Still Mystery

Why did Jason Lee's Mission Store near Salem pay Ewing Young $50 dollars for a kettle in 1838, at a time when shoes were selling for a dollar a pair and men's shirts were 60 cents?

This is a mystery that has never been solved, but the transaction was on the books of the Mission Store, and there is speculation that the exhorbitant

price was paid to remove the temptation of making alcoholic beverages from the Oregon scene.

Young was a trapper and trader who arrived in

Oregon after driving a herd of horses up from California. At first, there were rumors that the horses were stolen, but he was late cleared of the charge.

Arriving in Oregon, Young and a fellow named Carmichael secured a large kettle used for pickling salmon, and announced that they intended to produce "alcoholic beverages" for sale at a site near the mouth of the Willamette.

Jason Lee, a minister of the Methodist Episcopal Church and founder and leader of the Oregon Mission established near Salem in 1834, immediately organized the Oregon Temperance Society, and began circulating petitions against liquor sales. Then, he sent Young a friendly letter, along with the signed petitions urging that their liquor producing enterprise be abandoned. Lee offered to pay $60 for their equipment.

Young was impressed by the friendliness of the request, and promised to desist, but refused the $60 reimbursement. However, a short time later the $50 kettle transaction was recorded as payment to Young for a large kettle. Was it the same kettle that was bought by the Mission later, and was the purchase made to take the alcohol-making device out of circulation? ●

N.W. Visitor From Space

When Ellis Hughes discovered a 15-ton meteorite in the woodlot where he was cutting wood at his farm near Willamette in 1902, he thought it was a gift "from the good Lord."

As it turned out, the Oregon courts confiscated the gift, and Ellis was out a lot of time, trouble, hard work and expense.

But for a time, Hughes enjoyed national recognition as the possessor the largest meteorite ever found in the United States.

Hughes came to Oregon about 1890 from the coal mines of Wales via Canada and Australia. He married Phoebe Warwick, who cooked in a lumber camp at Linnton, Oregon, and had three sons. They lived on a 30-acre ranch which Hughes purchased from the Oregon Iron and Steel Company, located in the area that is today part of West Linn.

To make a living, Hughes cut wood for the Willamette School and it was on a wood-cutting trip in the forest surrounding his farm that he discovered the meteorite in the fall of 1902.

It was imbedded in the surface with the flat side up, and when Hughes struck it with his ax, it rang like a bell.

Because Hughes was worried that someone else would find the visitor from space and carry it off, he decided to take it home. This was not easy, as the 30,000 pound hunk of iron had to be moved almost ¼ of a mile.

By using his horses, cutting a track through the

woods, and using a series of winches, the family was able to get the meteorite safely to the backyard in the summer of 1903.

As news of the find spread, crowds from Portland and the surrounding areas began arriving at the farm. Scientists came from all over to view the meteorite and verify the find.

Even the Indians got in the act, they told of a "visitor from the Moon," incorporated in their legends, which led some to believe that the meteor had fallen within tribal memory. Other Indians told of having seen the meteorite when they were young and washing their faces in the rainwater in the puddles on its surface to give them luck. Others said warriors dipped their arrowheads in the rainwater before going into battle.

Hughes housed his treasure in a shed and began charging 25 cents per head for viewing. The Oregon Iron and Steel Company representatives visited and said the meteor had been found on their property and that it belonged to them.

The Circuit Court of Clackamas County found in favor of the Oregon Iron and Steel when the dispute came to trial. The verdict said, "We, the jury duly empaneled and sworn, find for the defendant, Oregon Iron and Steel, that it is the owner of the personal property described in the complaint, namely an irregular shaped piece of mass of iron probably of meteoric origin and that said defendant, Oregon Iron and Steel Company is entitled to the return thereof and we assess the value of said property at $10,000,000.

Hughes appealed to the Oregon Supreme Court and they upheld the decision of the lower court. Because he was not a citizen, he decided to drop the matter, rather than risk deportation.

The next summer, the Oregon Iron and Steel

Company moved the meteor to the Lewis and Clark World's Fair in Portland. Shortly thereafter, it was sold to a wealthy New York woman, who donated it to the American Museum of Natural History in 1936. Finally, the Willamette Meteorite found a home with the Hayden Planeterium.

Before it reached its final destination, however, it suffered the loss of several pieces. One is at the University of Oregon. Another piece is on display at the American Museum of Natural History.

Hughes went back to the hum-drum life of a farmer. He died in 1943.

For a time, one of his sons tried to keep the family memory of the meteor alive by building a replica of the meteor and displaying it at the family farm.

In 1962, another replica of the space visitor was dedicated in front of the Willamette Fire Station. The West Linn Fair Board published a booklet on the meteor, the same year. A display at OMSI in Portland, tells the story of the Willamette Meteorite, and laments that it couldn't be kept in Oregon. ●

Little Lady Shapes Up Town

Oregon's 14th governor, Oswald West, sent his 104-pound female secretary to subdue the wildest, most lawless town in Oregon after fearless sheriffs had failed to do the job.

West was a prohibitionist and the illegal sale of liquor was probably the most prevalent crime during his tenure, and the crime that he despised most.

Therefore, when the desert town of Copperfield in Baker County took the law into their own hands and issued themselves liquor licenses, West decided it was time for action.

Copperfield had a population of about 2,000 miners and construction workers at the time, and they crowded into the saloons to spend their hard-earned money on booze and gambling. After the town's incorporation in 1909, a saloon-keeper had been elected mayor and two of the three councilmen were bartenders.

Townsmen bragged that there never had been anyone arrested in Copperfield. Crimes were committed, but there just wasn't any lawman capable of getting a prisoner 150 miles to the county seat at Baker. The town rapidly gained the reputation as the wildest, most lawless town in the West until 1914 when the Governor decided that things were out-of-hand, and it was time to step in.

First, he sent 6'6'', 200-pound Ed Rand, sheriff of Baker, to clean up the town, but even Big Ed wasn't big enough to do the job.

Irate, the governor called out six national guardsmen, and sent them to Copperfield along with his personal secretary, pretty Miss Fern Hobbs, 25, who tipped the scales at 104 pounds.

Determined to get the boss's job done, Miss Hobbs marched into town and called a public meeting in the dance hall. She took the platform dressed in a stylish suit and read the proclamation issued by the governor calling for the resignation of the mayor and councilmen. They refused.

Miss Hobbs hesitated for a moment, and then read the governor's second proclamation placing the town under martial law. The guardsmen stepped up then and confiscated 270 revolvers, knives and other weapons. Then, they arrested the major and the council.

While awaiting trial, two of the councilmen tried to leave town on a freight train, but were intercepted. The mayor never came to trial because he was killed in a gun battle with another saloonkeeper.

Copperfield was subdued, and dead. A year later it burned to the ground. ●

"Grip" Was Forevermore

Northwest readers who admire the writings of Charles Dickens, or who have told and retold their children the story of Little Tim and Scrooge, will be interested in the story of "Grip," who was the author's pet raven.

Grip eventually became a "relic," but not before he inspired two notable literary works.

The dictionary gives many different definitions of the word "relic," but in the antique world, it refers primarily to objects that have specific known associations with notable persons.

Collectors frequently pay large amounts of money to take possession of historical relics or items which belonged to important persons, or person in whom they have a particular emotional interest. This kind of collecting somehow fills a deeply felt human need that crosses centuries and many civilizations.

As might be expected, there are many strange relics, and one of the strangest might be a stuffed raven named "Grip," which sold for $5,000, passed through several collectors' hands and finally came to rest in the Free Library of Philadelphia.

Dickens' Pet Bird

Grip belonged to Charles Dickens, who had an unusual devotion to pet birds. He owned several that spoke or sang, and he was tireless in writing to his friends about things the birds "said."

In one of his novels, Dickens used the raven as a "queer character" and gave him to the hero as a companion. Edgar Allen Poe, who reviewed the new

Dickens book in 1842, commented that the bird's croakings "might have been used to greater advantage and used prophetically in the drama." And three years later, Poe did just that in one of his poems, "The Raven."

In this celebrated poem, Poe's raven, no doubt inspired by Grip, croaked it prophetic "Nevermore."

Grip, having thus inspired two notable literary works, went to his reward on March 12, 1841, apparently to the relief of Dickens' family because he chattered constantly and also had the habit of biting ankles at random.

Mourned Raven's Death

Dickens, however, mourned Grip in characteristic fashion as he wrote to a friend:

"You will be greatly shocked and grieved to hear that the Raven is no more. He expired today at a few minutes after twelve o'clock at noon . . . on the clock striking twelve he appeared slightly agitated, but he soon recovered, walked twice or thrice along the coachhouse, stopped to bark, staggered, exclaimed 'Halloa old girl;' and died."

Dickens had the bird stuffed and placed in a glass case in his library. Grip was still in a place of honor when Dickens died in 1870. At the auction of the novelist's belongings, Grip was sold for the amazing $5,000 figure, and he was resold several times before he was bequeathed to the Free Library of Philadelphia by his last owner. ●

Oregon's First Auto Lost

Oregon's only automobile manufacturing plant was short-lived. It came into being in 1912 when it issued $300,000 worth of stock. When it went out of business five years later, two cars had been built as display models. They were about all that was left when the company took bankruptcy.

The company was the Beaver State Motor Company, and it had its "factory" in Gresham.

The bankruptcy proceedings took over 12 years, in the meantime, one of the two Beaver cars came up missing and was never found. The other, a "Beaver 6" was bought by the bankruptcy trustee attorney. His children drove it to school until the tires gave way, then they parked it behind their house.

There it sat until 1929, when the attorney said he was tired of looking at it and ordered it put on the bonfire and burned. The chassis was aluminum and the frame was oak. It burned just fine, and when the fire went out there was nothing left.

Exactly a month later, a man appeared at the attorney's office, checkbook in hand. He said he had been authorized by Harvey Firestone to offer $5,000 for the auto known as the Beaver.

The attorney was speechless, and his children declared that for the 25 remaining years of his life, he never threw anything away. ●

Clark Gable Rode Rails to N.W.

Clark Gable, on of the most poplar movie stars and one of the most repected male movie actors of all, got his real career start in little theatre in Portland, Oregon, where he also acquired his first wife. He developed some of his ruggedness working in the Northwest woods as a surveyor and as a logger.

Gable, even at the heighth of his career was pictured as a man who liked a simple life. He smoked a pipe with a brand of tobacco that cost ten cents a can. He liked dogs, horses and guns and his vacations were often camping trips in the mountains.

Clark Gable was 17 years old before he ever saw a city. He was raised on a farm and in a small town of only 500 population.

There was no sophistication in his youth, and he always was a little shy. Born in Cadiz, Ohio, his father, William Gable was an oil contractor. His mother died when he was seven months old, and his father, fearful that he could not care for the boy properly, sent him to his mother's parents in Pennsylvania. The boy spent his first five years on the Pennsylvania farm, with no near neighbors and no playmates. He learned to swim in the pond, and fed the squirrels in the hickory grove.

On Sundays, his grandfather would hitch the mare to the surrey and the family would drive to church at Meadville, the nearest town.

When Clark was five, his father married again, and Clark returned home, although at the time, he was reluctant to leave his grandparents. However, he and his new mother loved each other from the start, and got along well.

By this time, the headquarters of his father's operations had been moved from Cadiz to Hopedale, another little town in Ohio. The population was about 500, but to Clark it seemed more people than the world could contain. Here there were other boys to play with — dozens of them.

When he was eight years old, he was run over by a farm wagon, and the kindly old family doctor came every day to see him. So deeply was the boy impressed by the doctor — by the miracles his hands could work in making nothing out of pain — that he decided to be a doctor himself.

Through his high school years he kept to his goal, dreaming of medical school ahead.

He found time for athletics, however, and played on all the school teams — football, baseball, basketball and track. But he was an utter loss socially. He was awkward, shy; he never seemed to know what to do with his hands and feet. In the presence of girls he became a stumbling, stuttering, bashful hick.

Toward the end of his high school course, Clark's father bought a farm near Ravenna, Ohio, and tried to interest his son in farming. He did not have th money for medical school. But Clark never wanted to be a farmer.

"I'll work myself through medical school," he told his father. And his step-mother — the woman who understood and helped and encouraged him every day of his youth — stood behind him.

"You can do it," she told him.

So at 17, just after graduation from high school, he left the farm and went to Akron to find a job. He'll never forget that first hour in Akron. He'd never been in a city before, and for one solid hour he just sat in the station watching the teeming life through wide-opened eyes, afraid to venture alone into the hustle of the city.

But there was no turning back. There was only one way to go, and that was ahead. The very next day he found a job, as timekeeper in a rubber factory. He told them he was 20; they paid him the unbelievable sum of $100 a month.

That very evening he enrolled in the pre-medical class of the night school at the University of Akron.

He laid out his routine before him; all day he worked in the rubber factory, five nights a week he went to school.

The sixth night, however, proved his undoing.

In a tiny lunch-wagon that night he happened to sit with two young men from a stock company, playing in Akron. Actors. To Clark they seemed beings from another, unapproachable world.

He'd never been to a theater. He'd never seen an actor. Compared with actors, doctors were commonplace.

The two young men invited him to watch the show, backstage. Of all the experiences in the intervening years, that night in the wings of the little theater in Akron was the greatest.

For the first time he glimpsed into the world of make-believe; he saw the eagerness, the joy, the thrill that the theater gave them. No one doctor could do so much for so many people.

He knew then that he would never be a doctor. The only life for him from that moment on was the stage.

But the theater did not greet him with open arms. He was an overgrown, gawky country boy. There was no place for one like him on the stage. Nevertheless, he kept coming back, night after night. Finally the manager gave him a job, probably more to get rid of him. He was made a call boy, without salary. But that did not matter. He still worked all day at the rubber factory.

As the weeks went by he absorbed the lessons of the theater. He memorized some of the parts. He walked on the stage before an audience, and was not afraid. He learned the tricks of make-up.

And then came his grand debut! One night he spoke his first line from the stage. He was playing a butler. And his line was, "Good evening, madam."

After that it was but a short time until he got a real part. Not a big part but a beginning.

Then, just as life was dawning for him, the dark clouds gathered. One night, just before the curtain rose, he received a message. His second mother had died. He went on the stage that night with his eyes red from weeping.

As soon as he could, he hurried back to the farm. His father was broken-hearted. He could not stand the memories of the farm alone. He talked of selling it and going back to the oil fields. But even the oilfields were lonely . . . if only he had someone to go with him . . . .

That was the first time that Clark Gable forgot the road ahead — forgot the top of the ladder — forgot ambitions, dreams, everything. He loved his father.

"We'll go together, dad," he said. "We'll both go back to the oil-fields."

And he did. With his own heart broken, his future empty, his dreams an empty illusion, he gave up the stage and went with his father.

They went to Bigheart, Okla. From dawn to dark, Clark worked in the clanking roar of the oil fields, grimy and greasy from head to foot.

He stayed in the oil-fields for a year. By that time his father had found friends — his first overwhelming loneliness had passed. Clark went back to the stage. Almost at once, he landed a job as an actor in a little traveling theatrical company in Kansas City.

He traveled every town of the West, sometimes making a little money, sometimes dead broke. But he stuck. Finally in March, the company became stranded in Butte, Montana. It was still winter in Montana. It was bitterly cold. And Clark was hungry. Hungry and broke.

He went into a hotel lobby and wrote a telegram to his father. He tore it up and wrote another. He wrote nine altogether, and tore them all up. He would not admit that he had failed. That night he jumped a freight train going West. Next morning he was in Portland, Ore.

Luck was with him. Through a little theatrical agency, he landed a job with a fly-by-night company leaving immediately for Astoria, a small fishing town.

No salaries were paid; it was a profit-sharing proposition. In 10 weeks he was stranded again. He went back to Portland. Show business was in a slump. There were no theatrical jobs. But he had to eat.

He found a job as a rod man with a surveying party and for the next nine weeks plodded through the heavy brush of the forest country.

After that, there was a job at a lumber camp in Silverton, Ore., which lasted long enough for him to save the carfare to Portland. But still there was nothing in show business.

He found a job in the want ad department of the Oregonian. There was hope in this; at least he could see the ''help wanted'' ads before anybody else did. Finally he found a job in the telephone company that paid more money.

But the stage was still in his blood, the smile was on his lips, and the vision was in his heart. He saved his money carefully; some day, he told himself, he would have enough to go to Los Angeles. Then he'd make good!

He heard of a Little Theater movement popular in Portland. The manager was a clever young woman who also conducted a dramatic training school. Clark enrolled and spent every evening in the theater.

Here he received his first really professional theatrical schooling, for the Little Theater was managed as carefully as any metropolitan show-house.

He conceived a tremendous admiration for the young woman who conducted the theater and its affiliated dramatic school. Months later, in Los Angeles, she became his wife.

Finally he got to Los Angeles. But not to immediate success. There was no job on the stage awaiting him.

He said that he occupied every bench and every chair in every casting office in Hollywood. That's why he was always the greatest champion of the extra players. He'd been there.

Came his chance in the movies. As an extra, he was one of 12 soldiers; all he did was to stand still and hold a spear. But it was three days work, at $7.50 a day.

Because he was such a good soldier, he got a similar "bit" in the stage production of "What Price Glory." Then another lucky break. The man who played "Sergeant Quirt" left. Clark was given the role.

From then on, the road led steadily upward — with many another setback, to be sure — but upward. He saved enough money to get to New York.

His first New York role was the leading part in "Machenal." To Clark Gable this was heaven. For 12 weeks, he trod the boards, leading man in a New York show! To the country boy who had slaved in the oil fields and the lumber camps, starved in every town in the West, it was almost unbelievable. ●

Oregon's Twenty Mule Team

The name, "Twenty Mule Team Borax," familiar to every housewife in the 1920's and 1930's, originated in Eastern Oregon's high desert country, and it ushered in one of the Northwest's most colorful mining enterprises.

From 1898 to 1907, borax was commercially mined on the Alvord Desert in Southeast Oregon. In an area of hot springs and Hot Lake, the borax formed naturally on the hot surface of the desert. When an enterprising railroad employee heard about the "alkalai" deposits in the Alvord Valley, he came to investigate.

With another fellow who had been mining borax in Nevada, the pair purchased 3,000 acres of desert for a reported sale price of $7,000 and began operations.

Mining began under the name "Twenty Mule Team Borax Company," which was destined to become a household word, but because the partners did not register the name, a California Borax Company that did register it later won the litigation over the right to use the name.

After this, the Oregon company was known as the Rose Valley Borax Company, probably because of the wild roses which grow around the hot springs.

During their best years, the Oregon company produced as much as 10,000 pounds of borax a day. This was obtained through a boiling process to reduce the borax to crystals. About 30 Chinese laborers were brought in and two steel tanks were installed alongside Hot Lake. These tanks were filled with the 97-degree water from Hot Lake, which were then further heated with sagebrush fires while the borax mixture was stirred. The Chinese tended the fires, did the stirring and then poured the mixture into large galvanized crystallizing tanks. It took about six days for the boric acid to crystallize on the sides of the tank.

It was then collected, rinsed and placed in piles on the ground to dry. After this it was bagged in 90 pound sacks, and loaded on wagons.

From 20 to 24 mules were required to pull the heavy wagons to the nearest railway at Winnemucca. It was from these "jerk-line mule teams" that the original name of the company and the colorful mule-skinner tales came.

Old records indicate that the Chinese were paid about $1.50 a day for their labors, and were provided living quarters in the sod houses on the property. They worked seven-days-a-week, but were given time off to celebrate Chinese New Year.

The company was sold in 1902, and continued to operate until 1907 when it closed for good. Some reports say the operation ran out of nearby sagebrush to fuel the fires, and listed this as the reason for the closure.

Today, visitors to Hot Lake can still see a few remnants of the old borax operation. There are remains of a few sod huts, and rusting vats. Hot Lake is still hot, and is a favorite area for nesting birds in the springtime. ●

Sets Record

Outlaws and desperadoes became so bad in Idaho in 1863-64 that a man could not venture out alone without being attacked, robbed and often murdered.

This deplorable state of affairs climaxed when a Charles Allen was attacked about 200 yards from his front door, robbed and pistol whipped and left for dead although he recovered.

Outraged citizens, recalling many such cases, formed a 1,000 member vigilante committee with detectives in every mining camp, saloon and community. Operating in secrecy, they began a clean-up which resulted in 21 professional rogues being hung between December 1 and February 1, 1863-64.

Their actions were speedy and those marked for extinction were apprehended and hung within 15 minutes, according to reports in the Walla Walla Stateman and the Boise News.

One of those hung by the vigilantes was Henry Plummer, the sheriff of Virginia City, who was himself the leader of a band of outlaws. He was hanged early in 1864. When he was taken, reports say, he wept and begged for mercy. On his person was found incriminating evidence, including the names of 85 of his clan with records of their deeds.

Another well-known outlaw who was brought to justice by the vigilantes was Boone Helm, who the Portland Oregonian in 1863 said had killed several men in the mines. Helm was also suspected of murdering and robbing all members of a party that he started out with in 1858 on a trip from The Dalles to Salt Lake City.

The Rocky Mountain News of May 1864 said the vigilantes had hanged 27 persons before mid-March of that year.

●

Mt. Baker Blew Its Top

The May 18, 1980 eruption of Mt. St. Helens shocked a lot of people in the Northwest — but erupting volcanoes are not new to the area — Cascade peaks have been blowing their tops quite regularly in the past.

For instance, there were over 20 known instances of volcanic activity on Mt. Baker in the northern Cascades during the 19th Century. And, although written records were scanty in the early 1800's and there were few people to record events, Mt. Baker evidently acted much like Mt. St. Helens has recently.

Mt. Baker was discovered on April 30, 1792 by 3rd Lt. Joseph Baker, who evidently was the first white man to see it and record the event. Lt. Baker sailed his ship into Dungeness Bay in the Strait of Juan de Fuca and observed the peak.

Geologists say Mt. Baker had extensive lava flows and pyroclastic eruptions 8,700 years ago, according to calculations. Then, 390 years ago there were more lava flows, mud flows and eruptions of volcanic material, mainly pyrorene andesite.

The earliest observer record, written by an Indian who said he witnessed the event when he was a boy, was an eruption about 1810. This blast killed all the fish in the Skagit River, he said.

In 1843, there was another eruption, and a large ash flow that again killed the fish in the river. Neither of these events was witnessed by observers who could accurately assess their violence, but an old Indian later told mountaineer Edmun Coleman that 1,000 to 1,500 feet of the summit of Mt. Baker disappeared during the earlier eruption.

In 1853, a long black streak appeared on the mountain, which puzzled valley residents. In 1854, geographer and surveyor George Davidson was viewing the mountain through a telescope when an ash eruption took place.

In 1858, prospectors looking for gold up the Baker River reported widespread destruction on the lower slopes of the mountain, much like that recently reported at St. Helens. Whole forests were swept away, they said, and below that there was half-burned timber.

Another report in 1865 states that Mt. Baker had taken on a new appearance. The familiar shaped peak was much flattened.

Climbers in 1868, the first time the mountain was scaled, said the crater was belching nauseous, sulphurous smoke. They also observed that there was no ice or snow in the crater, indicating that Sherman Crater had been very hot recently.

The last "big" eruption on Mt. Baker occurred in 1880, when a large volume of smoke as well as an "impressive pyrotechnic display" took place. Observers said fire shot far above the mountain top.

In 1884, Mt. Baker was smoking again. Then, it seemed to quiet down for a number of years, until the 1970's when it stirred in its sleep, smoked and steamed a little and then settled down again. ●

Record Three-Day Courtship

He met the judge's daughter and her family on Thursday and married her the following Sunday to establish some kind of record for an early whirlwind romance.

The dashing groom, who was Joaquin Miller, express rider, lawyer, editor, judge and poet of renown, was one of the Northwest's most colorful and controversial characters.

Miller was born in Indiana in 1839, moved to Eugene, Oregon with his family when he was 13-years-old. He obtained most of his early education from his Quaker schoolmaster father, but was a restless boy and he left for the California mines when he was just 15. He lived with the Shasta Indians for the next two years and acquired an Indian wife. Returning to Eugene in 1857, he attended Eugene's Columbia College for a time.

After that, he taught school, studied law and was admitted to the bar in 1861. However, the hum-drum life of an attorney seemed too tame, so later the same year, he got a job riding Pony Express from Walla Walla to the Idaho mines.

Tiring of this, he came back to Eugene and in 1862 became editor of the Democratic Register, a publication destined for short life because of its pro-slavery sympathies.

While he was editor, though, he read some poems submitted by Theresa Dyer, daughter of Judge George Dyer of Port Orford, and Miller dropped everything to rush there to meet her. He arrived on

Thursday and they were married three days later.

Miller and his bride lived briefly at Port Orford until 1864, when Miller drove a herd of cattle across the Cascades to Canyon City. They moved there, and Miller established a controversial status in the area.

Some old time residents, writing in their memoirs, recall Miller as a rather shiftless character and a big bluffer. Some even suspected that Theresa, who also wrote poetry, composed many of the poems credited to her husband. However, Miller eventually became a Grant County Judge and was active in community affairs. When he later became famous as a poet, Canyon City acclaimed him and made his little log cabin where he and Theresa lived a museum.

In 1870, after their third child was born, Miller deserted Theresa and she later divorced him. In the 1880's, he married a third wife, Abbie Leland.

Miller's first book of poems was published in 1868 when he was still in Canyon City. It was not well received or very popular. When he left Canyon City, he visited Great Britain where "Songs of the Sierras" was published in 1871 by a London publishing house. This book made him famous over night. He returned to San Francisco in 1872.

However, he continued to be restless and his forays after he returned to America took him to Asia and back to Europe several times. He lived in New York and Washington, D.C.; was a newspaper correspondent in the Boxer War in China and in the Klondike; and was a conspicuous figure at the Lewis and Clark Exposition in Portland in 1905.

He died in 1913. Among his best known works are "Songs of the Sun-Lands" (1873), "Pacific Poems"' (1871) and "Columbus" (1885.)

Paddlewheel Express Popular

By Herb Yates

Nautical Society of Oregon

In the beginning it took a lot to make a man consider moving to our Northwest Coast. Spanish ships had reached Lower California in 1533-34, and in 1542 Cabrillo touched at San Diego and may have sighted southern Oregon. The prospects seemed so dim, however, that when the governor of California was told that the Russians had designs upon California his reply (freely translated) was, "Let 'em have it!"

It took Captain Cook's third voyage to show the value of the furs from the Northwest Coast, and even then the prospects of a voyage there were grim.

A New England skipper starting for the Columbia River around 1800 knew he had litle chance of seeing his family until some three years and forty thousand miles had passed.

Economically restrained from trading between the Pacific Northwest and China by their own monopolies, British ships took a less active part in the sea-otter trade than did American vessels, and on May 26, 1810, the Winships of Boston entered the Columbia to found a permanent post.

The Winship's efforts were defeated by a freshet and hostile actions of local Indians who had been making a good thing of acting as middle men in trade along the river. The next year saw the establishment of Astoria, which quickly became British, and presently the entire coast became a fief of the Hudson's Bay Company.

Depletion of the sea-otter herds and a depression in the Chinese market had much diminished American interest in the trade by 1825, and the HBC was left to the enjoyment of the Northwest for trade.

Occasional American voyages to the coast were less than lucrative, incursions by American mountain men into HBC territory discouraged, and the company neither wanted nor needed American settlers.

However, tiny sloops, schooners and brigs were soon poking bowsprits into every possible entrance along the Northwest Coast. The most important entrance in Oregon was that to the Columbia River, of which one of the Chatham's crew had written in 1792, "I must acknowledge that in going into this place, I never felt more alarmed and frightened in my life, never having been before in a situation where I conceive there was so much danger."

The writer's feelings were not misplaced: it was a dangerous entrance. The HBC had lost ships there by the 1840s, and that decade was to see the loss of the U.S. Navy vessels Peacock and Shark at the entrance, the first trying to enter, the latter to leave.

The Columbia was the grand highway to the hinterlands where the immigrants were becoming farmers and loggers, and it was necessary to ascend the river for a hundred miles to reach the first point where a landing could be secured. That wasn't easy either, as the Winships had discovered in 1810 when they spent five days sounding forty miles of channel, " . . . the ship making very slow progress up the river, as the passage was found to be very intricate, and the current very strong . . . ."

When Captain Norton brought his brig Sequin on the coast in the fall of 1849 his first attempt to enter the Columbia was frustrated by a gale which blew the Sequin nearly to Vancouver Island.

Beating his way back he brought the brig into the river in late November, but further progress was stopped by headwinds and currents.

Lots of Rain and Ice

Mrs. Norton, who was aboard, wrote, " . . . for several days, we lay surrounded by a sheet of ice, with heavy rain almost without cessation until it had raised the river to an enormous height . . . ."

The Sequin lay at anchor for four weeks, and Mrs. Norton noted, "For many days the river was nearly covered with this immense quantity of drift, and some of the largest and handsomest trees I ever saw torn up by the roots with all their green foliage passed so near as to become entangled with our anchor."

The brig reached Portland 65 days after entering the river, having spent four weeks at anchor and then making as little as one or two miles a day during the trip up the river.

River Pilots Provided

The Territorial Legislature made provision for bar and river pilotage almost as soon as it first convened, and steam bowboats eased the difficulties of the river passage.

Soon chuffing little steamers were running up the Columbia with portages around the rapids and falls.

On the Willamette tiny paddlers ran as far as Eugene and felt their way up the Tualatin and Yamhill rivers. In a roadless land water transport was all important, a fascinating part of Oregon's maritime history.

Deerhunters Find Gold!

In the Calapooya Mountains in Southwestern Oregon, about 35 miles southeast of Cottage Grove and 80 miles east of the Oregon Coast is the Bohemia Mining District. It covers an area of about six by eight miles and was the site of one of the richest gold strikes in the state.

The area, which in the 1860s was remote and rugged, is also the location for some of the most colorful tales in Oregon history.

The first major discovery on Bohemia Mountain occurred in 1863 when two men, allegedly fleeing civilization after killing an Indian, made their way north into the Calapooya Mountains.

While dressing a deer one day, one of the men, named Johnson, looked in the streambed and saw the glitter of gold quartz. The find started a small rush to the area. Because Johnson was from the old world country of Bohemia, and was called "Bohemia Johnson," the mountain was named after him.

Champion Assay Rich

As more mines were opened, the trails were widened into rough roads. These roads were so narrow that occasional passing places were built and the lead teams of the freighters wore bells to let teamsters know that another wagon was coming and to wait at the turn out.

The most impressive mine in the area, the Champion Mine, had its initial assay set at $30,000 a ton. Only "reliable" men were allowed in this mine. Canvas was spread on the floor and the walls were brushed down on it. One man who saw some of the rock said it glittered like a jewelry store.

It took two days of hard riding to get to Bohemia from Cottage Grove, and for the first few years, all of the mining equipment and supplies had to be hauled in by pack train.

For the freighters, it was a 3-day trip from Cottage Grove with one over-night stop at the Painted Post Ranch and one at Mineral. Extra horses were kept at both stops to add teams to the loads for the steep grades.

Turn of Century Town

As the population of Bohemia grew to more than 400 persons, a town of sorts sprung up, and a stagecoach carried baggage, passengers and mail to Bohemia, starting about 1899. The stage was a two-seated hack drawn by four horses. The ride was not always a pleasant one, however. After heavy rains creeks became swollen torrents and had to be forded, and fallen trees frequently blocked the road.

In 1902, after the citizens of Cottage Grove and the Oregon Securities put up financing, the Oregon and Southeastern Railroad became a reality. It linked Bohemia with Cottage Grove connecting with the main line railroad from Portland to California.

The colorful Oregon and Southeastern Railroad soon became known as "Old Slow and Easy," for its initials O&SE, and weekend and holiday excursion trains were soon the "in" thing for Cottage Grove recreation. However, the line was essentially a working train and a vital link between the back country and the bright lights of Cottage Grove.

New Trail Blazed

"God never made a mountain but what He provided a place for man to go around it."

A landmark in the great Oregon immigration of the 1840s and '50s was the Barlow Road, which brought westward-bound travelers from The Dalles south around Mt. Hood to Oregon.

Before the blazing of the trail, immigrants coming over the Oregon Trail to The Dalles were shocked to find that the downriver passage on the Columbia was not only relatively dangerous but the fee ruinously high, far more than the average family expected or could pay.

The Samuel K. Barlow family left Farmington, Ill., in March of 1845 with the migration of 1845 to the Oregon Territory. They joined about 5,000 others at Independence, Mo., where Barlow was elected captain of one group of wagons.

Arriving at The Dalles Mission the latter part of September, 1845, travel-worn and tired, the settlers were dismayed to find wagons, cattle and travelers everywhere. Food supplies were limited, and only two boats were running down to the Cascade Rapids. Charges were high, and there was an indefinite wait.

Facing this intolerable plight, Barlow, William Rector and others in the group decided to try to blaze a wagon road around the southern slope of Mt. Hood. Barlow looked at Mt. Hood, standing majestically before him, and declared, "God never made a mountain but what He provided a place for man to go over or around it."

With this determined spirit, he set out on Sept. 24 in a party of seven wagons, 19 adults, several children and about 50 head of livestock. There were no problems the first 35 miles, and they passed the present towns of Boyd and Dufur over open countryside.

The Barlow party descended a steep slope into Tygh Valley, where most of the group camped while Barlow and Rector went on ahead to find a possible route through the mountains.

While the men were gone, another group of 15 families and 23 wagons, headed by Joel Palmer, joined the first group. They had heard of the Barlow plan and wanted to go along.

The plan was formulated for the wagons to be left behind, a cabin to be built to store the belongings and for the party to proceed on horseback and foot to Oregon City. A cabin was built on Barlow Creek, about five miles south of the summit, and Barlow and Rector set out for Oregon City on foot to find provisions to replace the dwindling food supply.

They found travel very difficult, taking much longer than Barlow had anticipated when he stood on the slopes of Mt. Hood on his scouting expedition. Finally they stumbled into the camp of Philip Foster, who was building a grist-mill on Goose Creek. Foster took them to his house, where they ate and rested before continuing their journey to Oregon City.

Arriving at the Provisional Capital of the Oregon Country, they were refused credit at the American store and the Methodist Mission store. The Hudson's Bay Company store, however, gave them credit without question. They stocked up and hurried back to camp with the precious food supply.

On Oct. 16, Palmer, William Buffum and wife and Mrs. Arthur Thompson departed for Oregon City on horseback. On Oct. 19, they met a pack train carrying provisions to the settlers, donated by the citizens of Oregon City. Palmer, C. Gilmore and an unnamed Indian returned to the immigrant camp on Barlow Creek with the food while Buffum, his wife and Mrs. Thompson rode on to Oregon City, arriving on Oct. 22. Palmer reached the camp Oct. 20, and the settlers started leaving camp in small groups.

Winter had set in, and progress was slow. Snow covered what grass there was, and thick fog added to the difficulties. Many of the animals died from eating toxic shrubs, and the camps were generally cold, wet and uninviting.

The immigrants straggled into Oregon City a few at a time, until all had safely arrived, more than eight months after departing. Despite the many hardships, there were no deaths to mar the arduous trip.

When all had departed, William Berry remained at the cabin in the mountains, which the travelers called "Fort Deposit." He stayed through the winter until it was possible for the owners to return and reclaim their belongings.

After the long journey was behind him and the newcomers set about making homes in the new land, Sam Barlow applied for and was granted permission to build a toll road over the trail he had blazed. Philip Foster joined Barlow as a partner, and the road they built was instrumental in bringing settlers into the Willamette Valley before the advent of the railroads.

Passage was $5 for a wagon, although this later was reduced to $2.50.

The area through which the old Barlow Road passed is now full of homes, resorts and small communities, and vacationers now enjoy what the settlers of 1845 had once thought they would never escape. ●

Serenade to Moon probably saved Singing Smith
who was lucky enough to fall into tree.

Rescue of Singing Smith

Snow at the Bohemia Mountain mines in the Calapooya Mountains near Cottage Grove reached great depths in the winter, and most of the travel was by skis. The miners, who lived a lonely life with only occasional forays into town, were known to "hit the bottle" sometimes on these excursions.

One miner, Bohemia Smith, could go a year without taking a drink, but when he decided to celebrate, he did a bang-up job.

One time he started to Bohemia with a jug, according to a story among those gathered by the Writers' Discussion Group, which put together the book "Golden Was the Past."

When Smith didn't arrive at his destination on time, search parties went looking for him. One party heard him singing, but couldn't locate him.

Finally, they found him. In the darkness and under the influence of the jug, he had stepped off the edge of a cliff. A small fir had stopped his fall, and he was still in the tree — jug in hand, singing and waiting to be rescued. ●

Red Petticoat Proud Banner

A red petticoat, presented as an insult by angry pioneer women, became the banner flag of a company of troops from Fort Vancouver during the Indian Wars of 1855-56.

Later, when the irate ladies learned they had misjudged the young captain and his troop, repenting their hasty action and saying the original owner of the petticoat wanted it back, the company was obdurate . . . .

No. The petticoat had been given to them and their flag it would remain!!

It was a tense time at Fort Vancouver. Chief Leschi of the Puget Sound Indians had gone to war with the whites. The Puget Sound Indians and the Coweliskies from the area around Fort Vancouver were friendly, and it was feared they would join the conflict.

The Yakima Indians were attacking and killing settlers just 30 miles east of Fort Vancouver, and panic reigned almost every night at the fort, although no attack had yet been made on it. Someone would say the Indians were coming, and because most of the men were absent at the fighting front, the women and children would rush through the dark paths to the safety of the fort.

The Coweliskies were camped near the fort, and as long as they were nearby, the settlers felt they could be watched. But when the whole Indian camp was gone one morning when they awakened, everyone was sure they had gone on the warpath.

The young captain in charge of the troops

remaining at the fort felt that the best thing to do was to start out and try to find the Indians, learn their intent and try to persuade them to return to their campsite where they could be watched.

He found them about 20 miles north of the fort and negotiations got underway. At length, the Indians agreed to return to the fort with the troops the next morning.

But the plan fell apart when the sun rose and it was discovered that the Indian chief Umtux lay dead between the two camps. No one ever found out who killed him, or whether the murderer was a white man or an Indian, but battle lines were drawn and for awhile it looked like a full-blown Indian war was about to erupt in Western Washington and Oregon.

However, a shot was never fired. A French volunteer who went among the Indians to talk won back their confidence and they renewed their promise to return to the fort.

There was a stipulation, though. They wanted to be left free for 24 hours to bury their dead chief unobserved.

The captain of the military, fearing an Indian trick to escape without a battle, reluctantly accepted their promise and marched his men back to the fort leaving the Coweliskies to bury Umtux. (The place where the incident took place was later named ''Battleground'' — and remains the town of Battleground, Wash. — because it was the scene of the only Indian war confrontation in this area).

When the troops came marching back to the fort without any Indians, dead or alive, and no battle to report, the nervous women were irate and in the presence of an excited crowd presented the young captain with the red petticoat as a ''banner'' for his soldiers.

The young captain's face was white as he stepped

forward and on behalf of his company accepted the gift. In a terse speech, he added that the action of the soldiers was misunderstood, but said that if the company should be ordered to the front, their new flag would be carried into action. If carried into battle, he said, it would be dyed a deeper red before it returned.

The next day, the Coweliskies kept their promise and came marching in, putting themselves under the protection of the young captain.

The contrite ladies apologized, but the company kept the petticoat, and said it was proud to be the only military company of the war to be presented with a banner. ●

Built in 1883, the Round Barn in the shadow of Steens mountain in Southeast Oregon still stands as a reminder of the days when inland Northwest residents relied entirely on the horse for transportation. Not everyone agreed with the way the barn was used to break horses, but the method seemed to work for Pete French and his buckaroos.

Why Barn-in-the-Round?

A weathered monument of wood still stands, commemorating the colorful reign of Pete French, cattle king in the late 1800s in southeastern Oregon.

The Round Barn, located in a peaceful valley in historic Harney County, was built in 1883 north of the abandoned townsite of Diamond. The land then was known as a part of the old Diamond Ranch, which some years earlier had been added to the growing fiefdom of Pete French, manager and part owner of the French-Glenn Company.

During the years that French was acquiring land and developing the spread which was known by the brand of his first purchase, the "P" Ranch, located where the western slope of the Steens Mountain levels into the plain, he had three round barns "built in a style popular in early California so that horse breaking and training could continue unhampered by winter rains."

In 1970, the only one of the three still standing was turned over to the Oregon Historical Society. John Scharff, superintendent of the Malheur Wildlife Refuge, first negotiated a lease with the Jenkins Bros., owners of the old Diamond Ranch, putting the barn in the hands of the Historical Society. Later, when much-needed restoration and repair of the structure had been accomplished under auspices of the Society, the barn and two acres of its site were deeded to the Oregon Historical Society by the Jenkins Bros.

Although the conical roof of the barn needed

reshingling in 1970, having previously been re-roofed in 1918, the structural members were solid and strong. This, remember, was 87 years after it was built. They're still strong today. The gigantic central pole, 22 inches in diameter at its base, is 40 feet high, and like the smaller poles on the barn's perimeter, is of juniper — a wood almost as hard as iron which grows in the desert of Central and Eastern Oregon and Western Idaho.

When members of the Oregon Historical Society visited the barn prior to its acquisition by the Society, two great horned owls occupied a nest in the "pulpit" where the supporting members — also made of hewn juniper — fanned out from the center pole about 20 feet off the floor to the rafters above.

The barn is 100 feet in diameter to its outside wooden walls. Inside is a lava stone corral two feet thick, nine feet high and 60 feet in diameter. Between this wall and the outside of the barn is a 15-foot-wide circle paddock, under roof, used in the winter time for breaking and training horses. It is said that the Pete French outfit routinely broke 300 head of horses and mules each year.

Not all of French's neighbors agreed that his horse-breaking method, imported from California by French, was successful. Many contended that a horse broken under these indoor conditions, and apparently gentle, could spook when taken outside for riding.

An interesting sidelight is speculation about construction of the lava wall inside the barn. There is a series of square openings in the wall, about breast height, at regular intervals. Considering the sturdiness of the wall and the position of these openings, it is possible that French had in mind using the barn as a stronghold against the Bannock and Paiute Indians, who gave the settlers considerable trouble in the early days.

Before he built the barn, French had been involved in such warfare. In June, 1878, a large band of Indians led by Chief Buffalo Horn of the Bannocks swept in from around the east side of the Steens Mountain. They moved into Diamond Valley, the area in which the barn now stands.

Cowhands who spotted them raced to Diamond Ranch, where French was working with 16 men. He ordered the hands to return to the "P" Ranch, and then French climbed up on the roof of the hog house to cover their retreat. He held the Indians off, and then started for safety himself.

In the retreat, French's Chinese cook fell from his horse and tried to hide. The Indians found and killed him. French went on to Ft. Harney where a group of white settlers organized themselves and subsequently fought the Indians at Silver Creek. Chief Buffalo Horn was killed, and the remainder of his band retreated north into Bear Valley.

Many of the horses were needed by the French outfit for range work and the long annual market drive when cattle from the "P" Ranch were taken to Winnemucca, Nev., 200 miles away. Horses, and especially mules, were needed for regular delivery of supplies, too, mostly by wagon from Winnemucca.

Wood was a scarce commodity in Harney County, too. Willow, native mahogany, juniper and quaking aspen were standbys for building corrals, fences, gates, cribs, barns and shelters.

But lumber, for the round barns and for Pete French's comfortable ranch headquarters residence, the "White House," was brought in all the way from Canyon City, about 150 miles north, in the Ochoco Mountains. Wagons with 10- or 12-mule teams were the usual conveyances. ●

Oregon's trees are frequent victims when Mother Nature goes on rampage and big blow hits Northwest. In Portland in 1904, wind storm toppled downtown trees and wrecked houses, as storms have done before and since.

Mother Nature Pulls Surprises

If you don't like the weather in the Northwest, just wait a few years.According to the records, there has been a wide variety of weather conditions during the past 100 years, and almost anything can and has happened.

In 1894 and again in 1902, the winters were mild and balmy. Said one resident, writing to friends in the east, "We call it winter only because it is winter time." Another wrote: "In our Pacific States, we have no winter."

Again in 1906, the record says, "Every old resident of Oregon can recall more than on February in which peach trees bloomed and early spring flowers appeared on sunny hilsides, and when the roads were not only dusty, but the dust was warm enough for children to play barefoot."

Then, in sharp contrast there were the four times in 13 years when the Willamette River was frozen over at Portland — in 1875, 1897, 1884 and 1888.

Occasionally, the area has its drouths, too. There was the rainless autumn of 1863, when December found steamboats in the Willamette River aground. In the early 40's there was a February and March drouth and the rivers, creeks and wells ran dry before the downpour finally started the last of March. That summer, the area had the largest crop yield ever, according to early historians.

On the more violent side, Northwest weather really kicked up and produced the most severe storm ever known up to that time on January 9, 1880. It was a full blown hurricane, evidently much like the Columbus Day Storm of the 1960's.

A record low barometer reading preceeded the 1880 storm which came in from the Pacific Ocean on a Northeast course, leaving a path of fallen trees in its wake. Houses, sheds and barns were deroofed, signs were blown down in Portland as the winds cut a 1,000 mile path through Oregon starting at Klamath and

1894

The famous Portland flood. This is a view at West Park St. north from Ankeny St.

sweeping up the Willamette Valley.

Leaving Oregon, the storm took a course through Eastern Washington, destroying property from Spokane to Northeast Kootenai in Canada. Weather reports at the time said no storm of equal magnitude had ever hit the area before.

More localized windstorms, called cyclones or tornados, have been recorded on a number of other occasions. On January 15, 1887, Cottage Grove was hit by winds which ''picked up sheep, and demolished fences.''

Gervais had a wind on Feb. 3, 1881, which demolished buildings and uprooted trees. Weston was hit by a tornado on Jan. 21, 1900, which reportedly swept a 200-foot path through town.

Portland had a windstorm on Feb. 26, 1904 which ''wrecked several houses.'' ●

"Gentlemen" at Ft. Vancouver dined in style at table set with best British Spode, even though they lived in primitive Northwest wilderness. At far end of dining hall (under picture) is separate table where honored Indian Chief was allowed to eat in deference to his status.

Million Artifacts Tell Vancouver Story

Life in the Northwest was extremely rugged in the period, 1825 to 1845, but the "gentlemen" class who were the clerks and officers of the Hudson Bay Company managed to live quite elegantly, at least while they were stationed at Ft. Vancouver.

Ft. Vancouver was founded by Chief Factor Dr. John McLoughlin in 1824-25, as a fur-trading post and supply depot and it was the most important settlement on the Pacific Coast for the next 20 years.

Today, it is possible for visitors to Ft. Vancouver to get a glimpse of life as it was inside the fort, and contrast it to the hardships and conditions encountered elsewhere in this wild and unsettled territory at the time.

Ft. Vancouver was abandoned and closed by the Hudson Bay Company in 1860, after the Boundary Treaty between England and the United States gave everything south of the 49th parallel to the United States and left Ft. Vancouver in American territory. In 1949, the site became part of the U.S. National Pak System. Excavation of the site since that time has produced almost one million artifacts from the fort's past that has given a picture of the days gone by.

Five major buildings and the stockade of Ft. Vancouver have been reconstructed on their original locations. These include the bakery, wash house, Chief Factor's residence and the kitchen.

The Park Service also has a small museum at the site and an auditorium where a short slide show is presented.

A few of the million artifacts collected are on display, but most of the furnishings of the Chief Factor's house and other buildings are replacement items thought to be representative of their period.

These are things imported from England, as were the original items, which were all shipped around the horn and which originally took over a year in transit.

The most interesting of the antiques gathered for Showing at Ft. Vancouver is the collection of Spode, which consists of 4 patterns. Originally, there were about 40 patterns of Spode dinnerware used at Ft. Vancouver, according to Park Service information.

Spode was at the heighth of its popularity in England at the time it was used extensively on the table of the Chief Factor's house at Ft. Vancouver. Josiah Spode II had discovered how to produce "bone china" from animal bones reduced to a fine powder by heat. The result was the fine porcelain that did not discolor with time.

The designs of Spode china were mostly based on those of China's export porcelain which had been very popular in England, hence the "Blue Willow" and other patterns showing the Chinese influence. Later, Spode developed stone china, and then feldspar china.

To visit the Ft. Vancouver historic site, which is located in the city of Vancouver, Wash., turn east off I-5 at Mill Plain and then follow the signs to the visitor center on East Evergreen Boulevard. ●

Early N.W. "Mound Builders"

Did an ancient people known as "mound builders" and who were perhaps related to the builders of pyramids once inhabit the Willamette Valley and build the 87 "little pyramids" found in the 1800s near the Calapooia River?

Alfred Blevins, who came to Tangent, Oregon, with his parents in 1840, told of the mounds and related that in his boyhood, old Indians had told him that their oldest ancestors were not able to learn from those who had preceded them what the purpose of the mounds were, or who had built them.

In 1884, Blevins accompanied a doctor, a minister and several other persons to the mound sites on the Calapooia two miles west of Tangent, and the group made a "careful study" of several of the mounds.

They concluded after digging in the mounds for many days that a number of the mounds which they explored contained the remains of an ancient people known as "the mound builders." Based on findings of human bones in the mounds and elephant bones and tusks buried in the blue clay nearby which were in the same state of preservation, they speculated that the people who made the mounds may have been here when elephants, mastodons, and saber-toothed tigers roamed the country.

They also concluded that because of the presence of charcoal in the mounds, fire had played some part in the mound builders' funeral ceremony.

Later writers have suggested that "the following might be offered in defense of this conclusion: white men now bury their dead in the earth, but in Europe and other couuntries in ancient times, the dead were buried under mounds of earth and stones, or were entombed in pyramids.''

This leads to further speculation, supported by some ancient Indian legends, that the migration of people to the West Coast came from the East or South, where other pyramid builders lived.

Until recently, the idea that man might have inhabited the Northwest as much as 12,000 years ago — when mastodons and elephants roamed the country — might have seemed remote.

Now, however, the finding of human bones together with those of the saber-toothed tiger in the LaBrea deposits near Los Angeles, and the finding of a manmade spear point in the bones of a mastodon on Washington State's Olympic peninsula, indicates that man, the hunter, roamed the country 12,000 years ago. This sheds new light on the Calapooia findings, if they have been accurately reported. ●

Whose Kid is Whose?

There's a place in Eastern Oregon in the Umatilla River Valley called "Happy Valley," and it got its name back in 1868 because the people living their said they had such a good time.

Every Thursday night, everyone living within a radius of eight to 10 miles met at one of the homes for an evening of pot-luck dining and dancing. Most of the residents were former Missourians and had large families — 6 to 8 children — and they all came along. The youngest were dumped in two or three beds after supper.

"The only trouble we ever had at our dances was to find the right babies when we got ready to go home," one of the women remembered. It was said that some ladies lost their own babies and got others through mistake, recalled another old-timer.

"I wouldn't vouch for that being true, but there were times when I, myself, was in doubt that I had the right kid or not. But I didn't make any fuss about it for I knew the other fellow would get the worst of the trade," she said, writing in her journal later. ●

Chief Outwits N.W. Slicker

Sometimes the unscrupulous white man of the early West who attempted to defraud the Indian came out second best.

This is what happened when How-lish-wampa, chief of the Cayuse Indians at the Umatilla agency, cleaned up on a horse race.

Chief How-lish-wampa had a pinto cayuse pony sired by a thoroughbred that was one of the fastest race horses for a distance from five miles up that was ever bred in Eastern Oregon.

The Indian race course along the Umatilla River bottom was two-and-a-half miles long. At the end was a stake and the riders turned at this stake and returned to the starting point.

Joe Crabb, a white man, was owner of a horse that had beaten every horse that it had raced, and he wondered if it could beat the chief's pinto. So, he managed to get someone to sneak the pinto out of the corral one night and with a good rider on it, he raced it against his horse. There was nothing to it. His horse won easily, so the next day he challenged How-lish-wampa to a race and the challenge was accepted.

Whenever an Indian horse ran against a horse owned by a white man, the Indians out of loyalty always bet on their own horse. Joe Crabb knew this, so he taunted the Indians until many bet everything they owned on the chief's pinto.

On the day of the race, nearly everyone in the area was on hand to watch. The Indians turned out en masse. Joe Crabb had passed the word to his friends to bet the limit, as he had raced the two horses and was therefore positive the Indian horse didn't have a chance.

When the Indians learned that Crabb had stolen the pinto one night and tried the two horses, they seemed apprehensive, but How-lish-wampa, owner of the pinto, laughed and sent back to the reservation for more horses to bet.

As the racing horses lined up at the start, the stakes were heavy. In front of the bettors were blankets spread with great piles of $20 gold pieces. The Indians not only bet their money and their horses, but also their saddles and everything else they owned, rather than seem to go back on their chief and his horse.

Joe Crabb's racer was a blooded horse that shone in the sun, while the pinto seemed unkempt, and the Indian rider, a young boy, was naked except for a breechcloth, while the rider on Crabb's horse had silver spurs, a jaunty cap and a silk crimson uniform.

Crabb's horse made a good race, but was no match for the pinto. The chief's horse ran the 5¼ miles and 83 yards in 9 minutes, 51 seconds (a record up to that time). Crabb's horse gave up the race after running four miles, and the pinto swept to the finish along.

After the race, How-lish-wampa gave Joe Crabb back the saddle horse he had won from him and also gave him a handful of double eagles. He said, "Next time you steal my racing horse to try him out, be sure you get right horse. The horse you stole that night and tried out was half-brother of my racer."

How-lish-wampa won about $20,000 on the race and the Indians were rich for a long time afterwards.

●

Band, Casket Used in Fund Move

Being a banker in the early days in the Northwest was not always easy. Banks played an important role in the lives of the early townspeople, and many legends sprung up around banking episodes and about the men who ran the banks.

One incident which has become a legend is said to have taken place in McMinnville, Oregon in the 1880's. It seemed that a substantial depositor had a falling out with the banker at one of the local banks (no one is sure whether it was at the First National Bank or at the McMinnville National Bank). In any case, the man decided to transfer his fund from the bank that he was enraged at to the other bank, but he wanted everyone to know that the bank was losing one of its most substantial customers.

So, the angry plutocrat went to the town undertaker and rented a casket. Then he hired the McMinnville band, and on a busy afternoon, the angry depositor, the rented casket and the band were deployed to the front of the bank that had his account.

When a sufficient crowd had gathered to listen to the free musical concert, the depositor began to withdraw his funds in the form of "hard cash" in cloth bags. These he carried with a flourish to the casket, and then, accompanied by the band, the strange procession marched to the other bank. Several trips were made before the transfer was complete, with the band playing "full throttle" all the way.

Another story involving the Wortman Bank in McMinnville tells of a dead man that spent almost 20 years in the bank vault.

As the story goes, a family moved to McMinnville and established an account at the Wortman Bank, then the husband died. After the funeral was held and the body was cremated, the family decided to leave the area. Going to the bank officers, the wife explained that since the family had no roots in McMinnville, they would like to wait until they were settled somewhere before putting the ashes in a mausoleum. Would it be all right to store the ashes in the metal container in the bank vault until they could send for them?

The reluctant bank officials finally agreed, and the family left. Weeks went by, then months and no word was heard from the family. They seemed to have dropped from the face of the earth and the ash container continued to gather dust in the bank vault.

More than a decade went by and there was still no word from the family. Only after about 20 years had elapsed was the bank finally able to evict the "temporary" vault tenant. ●

Horse-drawn casket and town band were hired to
supply fanfare when Willamette Valley bank
depositor "of means" became angry at his banker in
1880 and decided to transfer his funds to rival bank.

Everyone in the city turned out to wave goodbye and all the tugs, boats and steamers in the harbor followed in their wake until they turned through the Golden Gate.

A First for Oregon Boys

The first expedition in the history of the United States to leave the country to fight a war of conquest included an Oregon company of troops. They were bound for Manila to fight in the Spanish-American War.

Oregon soldiers from Pendleton and LaGrande were known as "Company D" of the 2nd Oregon Regiment. They left on May 25, 1898. After a stop at the Presidio in San Francisco, they joined other companies and sailed out through Golden Gate with the biggest ovation ever.

Admiral Dewey's victorious fleet greeted them at Manila Bay, after a grueling 37-day ocean trip. Then, they spent a month at a deserted Spanish garrison at Cavite before they saw their first action when they were the first American soldiers to enter the fallen city of Manila. A color guard immediately hauled down the Spanish flag while the 2nd Oregon Regimental Band struck up "The Star Spangled Banner."

The Oregon regiment, which consisted of about 1,200 men, was in the Philippines until July, 1899. During that time, they participated in more than 20 battles and skirmishes. Once they were ordered home, then were again put in the field to dispel insurgents near Morong.

The regiment arrived back in San Francisco on July 14, 1899, to an even bigger welcome and reception than when they sailed. And two more heroes' welcomes awaited them - one in Portland and another when they got back to Pendleton. ●